SHERLOCK

**Every Canon Reference
You May Have Missed in
BBC's Series 1-3**

Other Works by Valerie Estelle Frankel

Henry Potty and the Pet Rock: An Unauthorized Harry Potter Parody

Henry Potty and the Deathly Paper Shortage: An Unauthorized Harry Potter Parody

Buffy and the Heroine's Journey

From Girl to Goddess: The Heroine's Journey in Myth and Legend

Katniss the Cattail: An Unauthorized Guide to Names and Symbols in The Hunger Games

The Many Faces of Katniss Everdeen: Exploring the Heroine of The Hunger Games

Harry Potter, Still Recruiting: An Inner Look at Harry Potter Fandom

An Unexpected Parody: The Unauthorized Spoof of The Hobbit Movie

Teaching with Harry Potter

Myths and Motifs in The Mortal Instruments

Winning the Game of Thrones: The Host of Characters and their Agendas

Winter is Coming: Symbols, Portents, and Hidden Meanings in A Game of Thrones

Bloodsuckers on the Bayou: The Myths, Symbols, and Tales Behind HBO's True Blood

The Girl's Guide to the Heroine's Journey

Choosing to be Insurgent or Allegiant: Symbols, Themes & Analysis of the Divergent Trilogy

Doctor Who and the Hero's Journey: The Doctor and Companions as Chosen Ones

Doctor Who: The What Where and How

This book is an unauthorized guide and commentary on the BBC show *Sherlock*. None of the individuals or companies associated with the television series or any merchandise based on this series has in any way sponsored, approved, endorsed, or authorized this book.

LitCrit Press
ISBN-13: 978-0615953526
ISBN-10: 0615953522

Contents

With special thanks to Yonatan Bryant and my brother Kevin Frankel, who kept asking when I'd do my 12th book of 2013 every single time I saw them. Guess this is it.

INTRODUCTION

There are thousands of Sherlock Holmes adaptations, from silent movies through the recent blockbusters. Endless fans have written original short stories, novels, and radio plays. Holmes and Watson have solved cases in the twentieth century, in space, in worlds of fantasy and wonder. Despite all this, Steven Moffat and Mark Gatiss have created something truly special with their newest adaptation, *Sherlock*.

As one critic notes:

> The writers most involved in *Doctor Who* and *Sherlock* are lifelong fans of both stories. Steven Moffat, who is showrunner on both series, would be the luckiest fanboy in the world if it weren't for Mark Gatiss, who is significantly involved in the scripting and gets to play a lead role on Sherlock, as Mycroft Holmes. (Penny)

It's not faithful to the exact details of the cases in the way the Jeremy Brett television show was – instead, Sherlock keeps the spirit of Holmes's methods while updating them – of course the famous detective who was "never known to write where a telegram would serve" would text instead of picking up the phone in the twenty-first century. "The original Sherlock Holmes was very much a man of the times, using all the most modern technology available, so obviously this one would be "intensely computer literate and very gadget happy," Gatiss notes ("A Study in Pink" DVD Commentary). Of course "The Greek Interpreter" might be a tale of comic book mayhem as the "Geek Interpreter" today. As Sherlock's fame grows in the books, it's mirrored in the eager fans swamping Sherlock for interviews and demanding he wear the garish trademark hat, much as fans actually do with Sherlock's actor. Moffat explains:

> The exciting thing about Sherlock Holmes is: an awful lot of the way forward is already there in the stories, 'cause we've already been quite faithful in a way to lots of the ingredients in those stories, but, you know, using them in new ways. What would "The Hound of the Baskervilles" be in a modern setting? What would "The Speckled Band" be in a modern setting? I just think, looking at those stories and updating them and thinking, you know, "What would a haunted house be?" ("Unlocking Sherlock")

Despite this departure from the original, devoted fans have noticed hundreds of references to the classic cases, and to the movies and more. Moffat mentions, "Sometimes those references are there as a joke, just for fun, or sometimes they're there because the ideas are simply good and untouched, waiting for someone to use them" (Adams 4). He adds:

> "Partly *because* we've committed this huge heresy of updating it, we sort of want to say to everyone who knows the originals, 'Look, everything else is incredibly authentic'. In fact, you'll never see a more obsessively authentic version of Sherlock Holmes than this one, because it is being motored by a couple of geeks." ("The Hounds of Baskerville" DVD commentary)

Moffat and Gatiss came up with the idea while travelling back and forth to Cardiff on the train while working on *Doctor Who*. Both discussed their admiration for the Basil Rathbone and Nigel Bruce films, which saw Holmes and Watson battling Nazis, dueling with swords, and operating in a modern world as well as a classic one, all while remaining true to the vision of the characters and their methods. Following this logic, the pair decided early on that everything on Sherlock Holmes was canonical: not just the stories but the Rathbone version, the Jeremy Brett version, and so forth.

Thus it can be difficult to track down all the references – Holmes appeared on film for the first time in 1900 in a silent scene produced by Thomas Edison. Since then, he has shown up in more than 200 productions. Some of those productions themselves, such as the Jeremy Brett series, contain dozens of episodes. Many fans have memorized the original short stories, but no fan could master this much canon.

As a devoted fan of both the classics and the new show, I'm attempting to share every reference with the fans of the show (or at least all the ones I could discover), mostly because I myself get such pleasure in spotting them all. Each one is a wink from devoted Sherlock fans Moffat and Gatiss to devoted fans in the audience – a way of sharing their love for the classic series while updating it for new fans in a world of texts, cellphones, and blogs.

SHERLOCK

A STUDY IN PINK

The Title

In the books, Holmes complains about the "romanticism" Watson adds to their first adventure when he publishes it "in a small brochure with the somewhat fantastic title of 'A Study in Scarlet'" (presumably referring to the violent murders and the message written in blood above the undamaged body).

"A Study in Pink" subverts and modernizes the story – pink is a cheerful, feminine color, and the garish look of the woman in pink from head to toe adds a lighter touch to the murder. Above all, it emphasizes that this story is a loose adaptation, not a retelling of the original tale.

The Story

The episode and "A Study in Scarlet" are notably similar, though with details often flipped or twisted. In both, Watson has just returned from war in Afghanistan as an army surgeon. He's looking for lodging, so his friend Stamford from St. Barts introduces him to Sherlock Holmes, seeking a roommate. Much of the dialogue is identical. Holmes of the books is a bit friendlier, but his priorities are much the same.

> "Dr. Watson, Mr. Sherlock Holmes," said Stamford, introducing us.

"How are you?" he said cordially, gripping my hand with a strength for which I should hardly have given him credit. "You have been in Afghanistan, I perceive."
"How on earth did you know that?" I asked in astonishment.
"Never mind," said he, chuckling to himself. "The question now is about hœmoglobin. No doubt you see the significance of this discovery of mine?"

Modern Sherlock asks a quick "Afghanistan or Iraq?" then returns to his case. Later, both detectives explain their reasoning:

The train of reasoning ran, 'Here is a gentleman of a medical type, but with the air of a military man. Clearly an army doctor, then. He has just come from the tropics, for his face is dark, and that is not the natural tint of his skin, for his wrists are fair. He has undergone hardship and sickness, as his haggard face says clearly. His left arm has been injured. He holds it in a stiff and unnatural manner. Where in the tropics could an English army doctor have seen much hardship and got his arm wounded? Clearly in Afghanistan.' The whole train of thought did not occupy a second. I then remarked that you came from Afghanistan, and you were astonished.

On the show, Sherlock notes:

I didn't know, I saw. Your haircut, the way you hold yourself says military. But your conversation as you entered the room...said trained at Bart's, so Army doctor – obvious. Your face is tanned but no tan above the wrists. You've been abroad, but not sunbathing. Your limp's really bad when you walk but you don't ask for a chair when you stand, like you've forgotten about it, so it's at least partly psychosomatic. That says the original circumstances of the injury were traumatic. Wounded in action, then. Wounded in action, suntan – Afghanistan or Iraq.

In both stories, Holmes is pleased to hear there's been a murder in Lauriston Gardens. Both times, he invites Watson to come and tells him about being a consulting detective – when the police are out of their depth, they call him. "Naturally, being the arrogant so-and-so he is, he'd had to give himself his own unique job title," Watson adds in his blog entries, available online for those seeking supplemental insights to the episodes (Watson's Blog, "A Study in Pink")

In both stories, Watson admires Holmes's deductions; on the show it's far more obvious that many people hate him for them.

In the book, a man has been murdered by being forced to take poison. RACHE is written over him in blood though he has no wounds. On the show, it's a woman in pink, and she scratched RACHE, not the murderer.

In the original adventure, a second man is murdered, stabbed, but with the pills left behind. Testing them, Holmes deduces the murderer has been making the other man choose a pill while he takes the other. As it turns out, the murderer, an American named Jefferson Hope, has come from America to revenge himself on the two men who killed his sweetheart. He makes them take the pills so God can choose the guilty and punish them.

Both this man and the modern "Jeff" work as cabbies (and thus get close to their victims, whom they murder in empty houses). Both murderers are terminally ill with aneurisms. In the book, Holmes calls for a cab, handcuffs the man, and reveals him as the murderer. The show has a more complex battle of wits, with Sherlock's own life at risk.

Certainly, in the book, there's no Moriarty or Mycroft, and Holmes and Watson are not in personal danger (though they are in many other cases).

Symbolism: Pink!

John Watson explains his titling, saying, "Well, you know, pink lady, pink case, pink phone – there was a lot of pink." "A Study in Scarlet" is renamed "A Study in Pink"…but what change does that create? Scarlet is of course the color of the splashed blood even at the violence-free crime scene (the first at least – the second involves an actual stabbing.

Pink by contrast, especially eye-searing electric pink, is a frivolous color, indicating the ridiculous, more modern and silly than noir. It's artificial, flamboyant, the shade of one desperate for attention. This is not just the dead woman but Holmes himself, as he shows off for all he's worth at the pink-colored murder scene.

Pink is a feminized color, one the cabbie fears as it will stand out and make him look ridiculous. Sherlock and Watson of course both fear looking ridiculous – for Watson, it's letting his life be taken over by Sherlock's wacky adventures, for Sherlock, it's loosening his rigid unemotionalism enough to make a friend. All their companions warn them they're in danger of being tainted forever by their association. By the episode's end, however, both have thrown out caution and embraced the madness of becoming a team. They've submersed themselves (metaphorically speaking) in a world of pink.

Blog

Moffat notes: "I think one of the fun things is, as you update it, as you find each equivalent...I remember Mark thinking, "Well, he wouldn't write a journal now, would he? He wouldn't write memoirs, he'd write a blog." And suddenly you realize, of course, that tells you what memoirs were. They were blogs" ("Unlocking Sherlock"). Thus John blogs about Sherlock's adventures and thus catapults the Great Detective into fame. This blog is actually available on the web at johnwatsonblog.co.uk, providing background information and John's emotional reactions to each of the cases, along with the tales of unseen cases references in "A Scandal in Belgravia" and "The Sign of Three."

> So yes, we had a quick look at the flat and chatted to the landlady. Then the police came and asked Sherlock to look at a body so we went along to a crime scene, then we chased through the streets of London after a killer and Sherlock solved the serial suicides/murder thing. And then we went to this great Chinese restaurant where my fortune cookie said, "There is nothing new under the sun. It has all been done before." After the night I'd had, I beg to differ. ("My New Flatmate")

This morning, for example, he asked me who the Prime Minister was. Last week he seemed to genuinely not know the Earth goes round the Sun. Seriously. He didn't know. He didn't think the Sun went round the Earth or anything. He just didn't care. I still can't quite believe it. In so many ways, he's the cleverest person I've ever met but there are these blank spots that are almost terrifying. (Watson's Blog, "A Study in Pink")

John, I've only just found this post. I've glanced over it and honestly, words fail me. What I do is an exact science and should be treated as such. You've made the whole experience seem like some kind of romantic adventure. You should have focused on my analytical reasoning and nothing more. –Sherlock Holmes (Watson's Blog, "A Study in Pink")

This last directly quotes the text of Holmes's reaction to Watson's write-up in the books.

Canon References

🔍In "The Problem of Thor Bridge," Watson mentions a couple of cases which most likely will never be cleared up. One is the case of "James Fillamore, who stepped into his house to fetch an umbrella and was never seen again" - That is also the name of the second victim in *A Study in Pink*, the teen who goes back for his umbrella.

🔍Watson and Holmes call each other by first names, which is a bit jarring. Even in *Young Sherlock Holmes* and *Elementary*, this behavior is unusual.

🔍John is from the Fifth Northumberland Fusiliers in both the episode and the original story.

🔍Anderson is named for the village constable in "The Adventure of the Lion's Mane," one of Holmes's last adventures, after his retirement.

🔍Sgt. Sally Donovan is from Sally Dennis, a fictitious character made up by the killer in "A Study in Scarlet" (there aren't many women's names in the story).

🔍Sherlock Holmes beats dead bodies with a stick and in "A Study in Pink" he does so with a riding crop (an oddly old-fashioned choice), in both cases to see how far bruises are produced after death.

In both stories, Holmes asks Watson whether he objects to a roommate playing the violin. He adds that he doesn't speak for days sometimes and that "Potential flatmates should know the worst about each other," in an adaptation of the original story's text.

Instead of going to the Criterion Bar, Watson and Stamford get Criterion takeaway cups of coffee.

When Sherlock borrows John's phone, he texts Lestrade that he should arrest the brother if he has a green ladder. (A reference to an outline for a Sherlock Holmes story found among Conan Doyle's papers.) Sherlock goes into more detail about this case on his blog.

Benedict Cumberbatch cites Jeremy Brett and Basil Rathbone (probably the most famous and iconic television/film Holmeses) as influences:

> There's a certain theatricality and ethereal spirituality to [Holmes] which Brett physically manifests beautifully; it's very animal, it's very cat-like and predatory and sharp and angular and slightly cold at times as well, and there are moments where I did want to use that. There are great descriptions of his physicality in the books as well, whether he's curled up on the chair with his feet tucked up so he's got his knees up and his hands on his knees and then the hands actually resting underneath his chin sort of in a prayer position. And I sort of wanted to play with motifs of that that people could recognize as being Holmesian because, without the pipe, without the deerstalker, without the old magnifying glass, it was important to establish certain codas and behavioral physical patterns that were recognizably Holmesian ("The Great Game" DVD Commentary)

The Jeremy Brett television series was adapted very little – each episode was meant to bring the book episode to life, nearly word for word. The Basil Rathbone ones mixed classic and original stories, and crossed in and out of the traditional setting. For instance, *Sherlock Holmes and the Voice of Terror* (1942) begins with a title card describing Holmes and Watson as "ageless," as an explanation as to why the film is set in the 1940s rather than Holmes' era of 1881–1914. At Watson's insistence, Holmes swaps his deerstalker for a fedora. By the next film, *Sherlock Holmes and the Secret Weapon* (1943), the detective is sneaking into Europe to save his country. This series takes much from the mannerisms of both detectives.

- Sherlock hops up onto his chair in a way very reminiscent of Jeremy Brett (in "The Adventure of The Empty House," among others).
- Sherlock has a website (which actually exists, like John's blog) called "The Science of Deduction." This the second chapter in the original "A Study in Scarlet" describing his methods after book-Watson finds his printed article, dully titled "The Book of Life." Oddly this is also the title of chapter one in Doyle's second book, "The Sign of Four," in which Holmes makes deductions from Watson's watch.
- Watson looks up Sherlock online and says disbelievingly, "You said you could identify a software designer by his tie, and an airline pilot by his left thumb?" This appears to be a nod to a canon quote: "Pshaw, my dear fellow, what do the public, the great unobservant public, who could hardly tell a weaver by his tooth or a compositor by his left thumb, care about the finer shades of analysis and deduction! ("The Adventure of the Copper Beeches").
- The lamps in Baker Street resemble gaslamps. Executive Producer Beryl Vertue notes: "It was interesting for everybody doing the interior of 221B Baker Street because, you know, we're not into gas lamps, as I've said to you. This is contemporary; this is modern-day, but at the same time you need – for the Sherlock Holmes aficionados – not to just lose it totally" ("Unlocking Sherlock").

The cluttered desk and mantelpiece, red walls, haphazard book piles, can all be seen in the Sherlock Holmes Museum on Baker Street today. Downstairs is a souvenir shop, not a café.

Of course, Sherlock keeps the sitting room in a terrible mess. His chemicals have been moved to the kitchen. Watson notes in the books:

> An anomaly which often struck me in the character of my friend Sherlock Holmes was that, although in his methods of thought he was the neatest and most methodical of mankind, and although also he affected a certain quiet primness of dress, he was none the less in his personal habits one of the most untidy men that ever drove a fellow-lodger to distraction. Not that I am in the least conventional in that respect myself. The rough-and-tumble work in Afghanistan, coming on the top of a natural Bohemianism of disposition, has made me rather more lax than befits a medical man. But with me there is a limit, and when I find a man who keeps his cigars in the coal-scuttle, his tobacco in the toe end of a Persian slipper, and his unanswered correspondence transfixed by a jack-knife into the very centre of his wooden mantelpiece, then I begin to give myself virtuous airs. ("The Musgrave Ritual")

There's a running joke about organs in the fridge and microwave. Watson mentions in the books: "Our chambers were always full of chemicals and of criminal relics which had a way of wandering into unlikely positions, and of turning up in the butter-dish or in even less desirable places" ("The Musgrave Ritual").

In the books, Holmes doesn't keep a skull around, but Sherlock appears to use it as just a head to listen to – on the show he tells John he's a replacement for the skull. In fact, Holmes enjoys talking aloud to solve cases in both stories.

Mark Gatiss notes in a DVD special:

> We were dressing various things in, and I spotted this picture, just there where it is now, and in the original stories Doctor Watson has an unframed picture of a man called Henry Ward Beecher. (He points to the picture.) This is not Henry Ward Beecher, but it's a complete coincidence. The props people had just dressed in an unframed picture and I said, "Oh, leave that; that's like a little accidental reference," you know. Um...and obviously through there in the kitchen, which Sherlock has just completely converted into his laboratory, we've got a lot of microscope equipment and test tubes and stuff like that. ("Unlocking Sherlock")

- The three-patch problem is an update on the "three pipe problem" ("The Adventure of the Red-Headed League"). Benedict Cumberbatch notes that it would have looked strange if he had been smoking a pipe on the show and that he wants to maintain the message that "cigarettes are bad for you" ("The Great Game" DVD Commentary)

- Modern Holmes has given up drugs and smoking (though continues with patches and skipping meals). He notes, "Impossible to sustain a smoking habit in London these days. Bad news for brain work."

- In the other modern retelling, *Elementary*, Sherlock Holmes is recovering from drugs and cigarettes. Cellphones, corporate crime, blogs, hacking, etc. feature heavily in both series.

- Mrs. Hudson is the housekeeper in the books and appears to be a genteel widow. In the show, she insists constantly she's *not* the housekeeper, and she owes Holmes for making sure her husband was condemned to death.

- Mrs. Hudson mentions "Mrs. Turner next door." Doyle accidentally renamed Mrs. Hudson "Mrs. Turner" in "A Scandal in Bohemia." On the blog, Mrs. Hudson often posts from Mrs. Turner's account, adding to the confusion.

Sherlock in both versions keeps his unopened letters on the mantelpiece, affixed by a knife.

Watson says in the books he has no family in England (many fans have added the facts of his "three continents" of experience with women and concluded he was born in Australia). Modern Sherlock observes that Watson clearly has no close relatives he likes.

Watson's wound switches between shoulder and leg in the books (Doyle wasn't the most consistent). On the show, Watson was shot in the shoulder but has a psychosomatic leg injury.

In "A Study in Pink," John receives three text messages from Sherlock:

> Baker Street. Come at once if convenient. SH
> If inconvenient, come anyway. SH
> Could be dangerous. SH

This is straight from the book: "It was one Sunday evening early in September of the year 1902 that I received one of Holmes's laconic messages: 'Come at once if convenient - if inconvenient come all the same – S.H.'" ("The Adventure of the Creeping Man").

Mycroft's aide ignores Watson. In the books, however, Watson's implied to be something of a ladies man: In "The Adventure of the Retired Colourman," Holmes tells his friend, "With your natural advantages, Watson, every lady if your helper and accomplice."

"You should come down and meet the Mrs. Just remember she's mine, Casanova!" – Bill Murray (Watson's Blog, "Serial Suicides"). Thus Watson's war buddy (Murray saved his life in the books) reminds viewers Watson really is a ladies' man. Harry is skeptical, but Bill adds, "The things he got up to before we went out to A. Dirty boy!" Perhaps he's just having an off year.

> Holmes was certainly not a difficult man to live
> with. He was quiet in his ways, and his habits were
> regular. It was rare for him to be up after ten at
> night, and he had invariably breakfasted and gone

> out before I rose in the morning. Sometimes he spent his day at the chemical laboratory, sometimes in the dissecting-rooms, and occasionally in long walks, which appeared to take him into the lowest portions of the City. Nothing could exceed his energy when the working fit was upon him; but now and again a reaction would seize him, and for days on end he would lie upon the sofa in the sitting-room, hardly uttering a word or moving a muscle from morning to night. On these occasions I have noticed such a dreamy, vacant expression in his eyes, that I might have suspected him of being addicted to the use of some narcotic, had not the temperance and cleanliness of his whole life forbidden such a notion.

Television Sherlock is far more annoying, dragging Watson across the city because he can't bear to get up. On the show, as in the book passage above, Watson is surprised to learn the disciplined Holmes takes drugs.

Mrs. Hudson says their glee over the homicides isn't "decent"; Watson likewise comments, "I can hardly think that you would find many decent citizens to agree with you" ("The Adventure of the Norwood Builder") when Holmes complains about his recent boredom.

Holmes says "The game is afoot!" in "The Adventure of the Abbey Grange" and Watson thinks it in "The Adventure of Wisteria Lodge." It's one of Holmes's most famous expressions. Here, Sherlock says, "The game is on," for the first of several times. This will also nod to "The Game is Back On" in "Many Happy Returns."

Mycroft is described here with the words "He *is* the British government," a line from "The Adventure of the Bruce-Partington Plans" that will be repeated through the show. In the books, Mycroft coordinates departments with his massive brain and is indispensable though not necessarily that powerful. In the creators' beloved *The Private Life of Sherlock Holmes* (1970) however, Mycroft heads many secret projects, as he does in this show.

🔎 Sherlock calls Mycroft "The most dangerous man you've ever met, and not my problem right now." In the books, he calls Moran, Moriarty's lieutenant, "The second most dangerous man in London" – Sherlock had appeared to be the first, but it could in fact be Mycroft. ("The Adventure of the Empty House")

🔎 Mycroft's three-piece suit and malacca-handled umbrella may nod to John Steed from *The Avengers*. As Mycroft leans on the umbrella and crosses one leg behind the other, he mimics Steed's mannerisms. This emphasizes his role as spy and government agent.

🔎 Mycroft says, "If you do choose to move into two hundred and twenty-one B..." which is a line a character played by Charles Kay says in the Jeremy Brett series.

🔎 The establishing shot of Baker Street and the layout of Sherlock's furniture are modern day versions of the Jeremy Brett scenes.

🔎 Angelo's helper is named Billy. This is Sherlock's "page" in "The Adventure of the Mazarin Stone."

🔎 The scene in which the police dismiss the dying woman's message mirrors a scene in *The Woman in Green* (1945) where a victim clutches a matchbook as a clue. Likewise, in *The Woman in Green,* Moriarty sponsors a series of murders when he arranges mysterious deaths across London.

🔎 A murder victim scratches a message in "The Adventure of the Retired Colourman" – in this and "A Study in .Pink," Holmes emphasizes putting himself in the victim's place.

🔎 In the books, the detectives are sure RACHE is short for Rachel, and Holmes remarks it means revenge in German and is frequently used by secret societies...however, the letters don't have a German flourish to them, so he's sure it's a false clue. On the show of course it's reversed – the detectives think it's "Revenge," but Holmes concludes it is the name Rachel.

"No, she was writing an angry note in German. Of course she was writing Rachel!" he says sarcastically.

🔸The woman in pink's wedding ring gives Sherlock several vital clues. Likewise, a wedding ring is the basis of the killer's motivation in the original "A Study in Scarlet."

🔸The men follow a cab in "Hound of the Baskervilles," and in "The Sign of Four," Holmes reveals that he always knows where he's being taken.

🔸Cabs and guns follow the pair through all of their stories, mostly because they use those in canon. Nowadays, firearms are illegal, and Holmes and Watson might logically take the bus through London. But the producers decided to keep these essential Holmes attributes. Steven Moffat notes:

> Now, you really wouldn't be running round London [with a gun]; you wouldn't be allowed! Also, we never actually say how he got that gun; it's just there. It's one of those marvelous things you can do in television: you say, 'He's got a gun,' and it doesn't seem incredible that a military man would have one. Maybe not supposed to have it but he's got it. ("A Study in Pink" DVD Commentary)

🔸The American cab driver Holmes catches is innocent because he's recently come to London – in the book, an American is the murderer.

🔸In the book, Holmes advertises using Watson's name to lay a trap for the murderer – that he has a lost ring. On the show, he sends a similar text but that the victim is still alive. Both times, the villain escapes by using another person as a decoy.

🔸Irene Adler says in her short story, "I had been warned against you months ago. I had been told that if the King employed an agent it would certainly be you. And your address had been given me." The cabbie is in the same situation.

🔸Mycroft has a joke with the audience as he introduces himself as Sherlock's "Archenemy" and wordlessly suggests he's Moriarty. He's far thinner than typical Mycrofts – one short story by Neil Gaiman sees Mycroft dying in his upstairs flat and his body being hoisted out and lowered like a piano. Thus as he wants to keep an eye on Sherlock, the viewers are fooled. This isn't as big a twist as *Elementary*'s unique spin on Moriarty, but it's big enough.

- Moriarty tells Holmes in "The Final Problem," "You stand in the way not merely of an individual, but of a mighty organization, the full extent of which you, with all your cleverness, have been unable to realize. You must stand clear, Mr. Holmes, or be trodden under foot."

> JEFF: You're not the only one to enjoy a good murder. There's others out there just like you, except you're just a man...and they're so much more than that.
> SHERLOCK: What d'you mean, more than a man? An organization? What? ("A Study in Pink")

- Sherlock tries luring the villain to Northumberland Street. This street and Northumberland Hotel appear in "The Illustrious Client," "The Adventure of the Noble Bachelor," and "The Hound of the Baskervilles."
- Holmes prefers texting to calling. In "The Adventure of the Devil's Foot," Watson notes, "He has never been known to write where a telegram would serve."
- Watson no longer lounges lazily about the house for weeks (as in the books), but is undergoing counseling for his admittedly psychosomatic injury, and blogs as therapy not an eagerness to sensationalize his colleague's mysteries.
- The shock blanket at the end mirrors Sherlock's iconic cape when he stands up.
- The running joke that Holmes would make a wonderful criminal is treated more seriously in the modern version, in which Officer Donovan and Watson express honest concern that this antisocial behavior and constant arrogance will lead to murder. Holmes calls himself "a

high-functioning sociopath not a psychopath" – while the Victorian gentleman was considered eccentric with his cocaine, solitude, and lack of friends, the modern detective acknowledges his social failings.

🔹Sherlock appears oblivious to the signals he's giving off and should be receiving – when Molly Hooper asks him about going out for coffee, he requests some, treating her as his secretary. In *Sherlock Holmes and the Leading Lady* (1991), Holmes is just as oblivious, inviting Irene Adler back to his hotel room just so he can have her try on a coat that's evidence in a case. When she says a gentleman would escort her out, Holmes assigns Watson to the job.

🔹Watson saves the day with his trusty army revolver – he brings it along in many stories and is sometimes forced to fire.

🔹In "The Sign of Four," Watson offers Holmes his watch as a friendly quiz:

> "Subject to your correction, I should judge that the watch belonged to your elder brother, who inherited it from your father."
>
> "That you gather, no doubt, from the H. W. upon the back?"
>
> "Quite so. The W. suggests your own name. The date of the watch is nearly fifty years back, and the initials are as old as the watch: so it was made for the last generation. Jewelry usually descents to the eldest son, and he is most likely to have the same name as the father. Your father has, if I remember right, been dead many years. It has, therefore, been in the hands of your eldest brother."
>
> "Right, so far," said I. "Anything else?"
>
> "He was a man of untidy habits, – very untidy and careless. He was left with good prospects, but he threw away his chances, lived for some time in poverty with occasional short intervals of prosperity, and finally, taking to drink, he died. That is all I can gather."
>
> ...
>
> "But it was not mere guess-work?"

"No, no: I never guess. It is a shocking habit, – destructive to the logical faculty. What seems strange to you is only so because you do not follow my train of thought or observe the small facts upon which large inferences may depend. For example, I began by stating that your brother was careless. When you observe the lower part of that watch-case you notice that it is not only dinted in two places, but it is cut and marked all over from the habit of keeping other hard objects, such as coins or keys, in the same pocket. Surely it is no great feat to assume that a man who treats a fifty-guinea watch so cavalierly must be a careless man. Neither is it a very far-fetched inference that a man who inherits one article of such value is pretty well provided for in other respects." I nodded, to show that I followed his reasoning.

"It is very customary for pawnbrokers in England, when they take a watch, to scratch the number of the ticket with a pin-point upon the inside of the case. It is more handy than a label, as there is no risk of the number being lost or transposed. There are no less than four such numbers visible to my lens on the inside of this case. Inference, – that your brother was often at low water. Secondary inference, – that he had occasional bursts of prosperity, or he could not have redeemed the pledge.

Finally, I ask you to look at the inner plate, which contains the key-hole. Look at the thousands of scratches all round the hole, – marks where the key has slipped. What sober man's key could have scored those grooves? But you will never see a drunkard's watch without them. He winds it at night, and he leaves these traces of his unsteady hand.

Episode one updates this to a cellphone, but the drunken charging (updated from winding), careless scratching, expense, gift from the older sibling, etc. are all intact. There's one catch, Watson tells Sherlock – Harry is short for Harriet.

"Across the road, we saw a taxi pull up. We ran out, but it drove off. Sherlock insisted on chasing it and luckily he seemed to have an intimate knowledge of London's backstreets. Of course, as I realized afterwards, he's probably memorized the London A-Z" (Watson's Blog, "A Study in Pink"). This last line of course foreshadows the cypher of "The Blind Banker."

Pop Culture

🥾 Steven Moffat notes: "The moment you bring it up to date, you...it sort of becomes half the familiar Baker Street and half "Men Behaving Badly" because that's what it is: it is these two fellas living in a flat, putting dreadful things in the fridge." ("Unlocking Sherlock")

🥾 The typeface used in the overlays is Johnston Sans, well-known for its use in the London Underground.

🥾 Apparently Molly introduced Moriarty to *Glee*. (Molly Hooper's Blog)

Innuendo

🥾 Holmes doesn't confirm whether he's gay or straight, leaving the fandom to speculate. He also, in an awkward moment, thinks Watson is asking him out. He responds, "John, you should know that I consider myself married to my work, and while I'm flattered by your interest, I'm really not looking for any kind of..."

🥾 At the time the original stories were written, Watson and Holmes were considered bachelors providing each other with company until Watson's marriage. Fan speculation about homosexuality comes from a more modern lens. On the other hand, some adaptations such as *The Private Life of Sherlock Holmes* (1970) emphasize that there could have been Victorian-era speculation about the pair.

🥾 John, on his blog gushes for some time about Sherlock and how irritating, fascinating, etc., he finds him. The girlfriends he dates through the series barely rate a mention.

MRS HUDSON (pointing upwards): There's another bedroom upstairs...(she winks)...if you'll be needing two bedrooms.
JOHN: Well, of course we'll be needing two.
MRS HUDSON: Oh, don't worry; there's all sorts round here. Mrs. Turner next door's got married ones. ("A Study in Pink")

ANGELO: Anything on the menu, whatever you want, free. All on the house, you and your date.
SHERLOCK (to John): Do you want to eat?
JOHN (to Angelo): I'm not his date. ("A Study in Pink")

MYCROFT: What is your connection to Sherlock Holmes?
JOHN: I don't have one. I barely know him. I met him...yesterday.
MYCROFT: Hmm, and since yesterday you've moved in with him and now you're solving crimes together. Might we expect a happy announcement by the end of the week?

Locations

🔺 The actual address used for filming the exteriors of 221B Baker Street is 187 North Gower Street, London NW1. There was a possibility of filming in Baker Street, but Mark Gatiss notes that "it would have been madness, apart from the fact that you would have had to disguise a hundred thousand things with 'Sherlock Holmes' on them," and the road was just too busy. ("The Great Game" DVD Commentary)

🔺 Speedy's Cafe, which is a genuine sandwich bar, exists on site, with Sherlock-flavored menu items.

🔺 The ancient Saint Bartholomew's Hospital appears in most episodes. (Once a medical treatment center, it's now an actual research facility.) Holmes and Watson meet here in both the original and "A Study in Pink." This is also the site of his Reichenbach Fall.

🔺 Sherlock's friend Angelo's restaurant was called Tierra Brindisa at the time of filming – now it's Tapas Brindisa Soho.

🔺 Scotland Yard, so famous in the stories, still exists, though it's moved from the street Great Scotland Yard. The Metropolitan Police Force work there, and its database runs on a nationwide IT system named the "Home Office Large Major Enquiry System" or HOLMES for short. The software training program is named Elementary.

Actor Allusions

Martin Freeman begins the first episode is in a dressing gown and pajamas. He dressed similarly in *The Hitchhiker's Guide to the Galaxy* movie. In both roles, he played a normal British man being dragged along on wild, larger-than-life adventures by a near-lunatic. Of course, this also describes his role in *The Hobbit*. Cumberbatch gets a promotion as Smaug and the Necromancer.

Doctor Who

🔺 The first actor to audition for John Watson was Matt Smith who, of course, went on to take a role in *Doctor Who* instead. They auditioned several very good actors but the moment they put Martin with Benedict, it changed Benedict and the way he played the role. "He was suddenly *more* like Sherlock Holmes," says Moffat ("A Study in Pink" DVD Commentary).

🔺 Many filming locations like the art museum of "The Blind Banker" or the cemetery of Holmes's grave are also used on *Doctor Who*. Both shows are actually filmed in Cardiff, except when location shots are used.

🔺 David Tennant's Doctor and Jack Harkness are both known for their ultra-cool long coats.

Sherlock asks John and Lestrade what it's like to live inside such tiny minds in "A Study in Pink." In Moffat's *Doctor Who* episode "The Doctor Dances," the Doctor asks Rose Tyler and Jack Harkness almost the exact same question.

THE UNAIRED PILOT

The Original Pilot Versus the First Episode

"A Study in Pink" on BBC's *Sherlock* is fascinatingly different from the original pilot version, as it caters to a modern audience's need for a complex story and tortured hero. The style, too, is different, using dramatic short cuts with text that compels the audience to pay close attention.

In the original pilot, Holmes lists out the clues he finds on the body, like the dirty jewelry. The first episode instead shows viewers Holmes's deductions with text. As the text floats around people's features, it's as if the audience is reading the clues as Holmes does. There's more snarkiness, as murders and Holmes's attitude are introduced in a press conference, with Sherlock's constant texts of "wrong!" Holmes is more self-aware, calling himself a "High-functioning sociopath, not a psychopath" while the pilot doesn't differentiate:

> LESTRADE: We're after a psychopath.
> ANDERSON: So we're bringing in another psychopath to help?!
> LESTRADE: If that's what it takes.

Sherlock takes pains in the first episode to reassure John that he's not the murderer, just because he has the woman's suitcase.

When adapting the pilot, the producer increased the mystery of the story, making viewers work harder to interpret the clues for themselves. "Rache" has been added. In the pilot, Holmes instantly deduces the murderer drives a cab, but in the first episode, he only wonders how the murderer can hide in plain sight, allowing us to make the deduction. In the second version, Sherlock fails to catch the taxi driver on the first try – only an innocent in the car. Likewise, the serial killer's assurance that his words cause suicides offers a puzzle Sherlock can't resist, and offers the viewers a long interval to figure it out.

In the pilot, the confrontation scene takes place at 221B, but the producers decided they wanted to explore more of London and so they expanded outward ("A Study in Pink" DVD Commentary). The flat is much less red and Victorian than it was in the pilot. Also, the set designers got rid of the split-levels because everyone kept tripping ("A Study in Pink" DVD Commentary). The original pilot was an hour, expanded to an hour and a half. Moffat notes:

> One of the advantages of making a pilot is that you can make the series right. That means you can look at a pilot and a pilot is changeable. You can alter it. You can say, "Let's change that set; let's alter that location," you can say any of those things. It might seem wasteful; it truly isn't. It's...the biggest saving you can make is to have, in effect, a test flight and see what this show looks like if it's actually made, as opposed to...as opposed to the theory. ("Unlocking Sherlock")

The first episode casts Sherlock as his own worst enemy, deepening the character and emphasizing the struggle he will have with himself throughout the series. The killer taunts him with boredom and drug addiction. As Holmes, not drugged or at gunpoint, nearly takes the pill, Watson shoots to save Holmes from himself, not the killer as he does in the original pilot.

The pilot, with its long psychological battle between hero and villain, focuses on character rather than mystery. Even the challenge itself – is offering the pill a bluff or double bluff or triple bluff? – focuses on the killer's character rather than any clues offered to the viewers. The killer dies, ending the threat completely for a happy ending as the camera fades out on Watson and Holmes' budding friendship.

Episode one, by contrast, begins a story arc, like most 21st century shows. Moriarty has masterminded the episode's crime, giving Holmes a season-long enemy to face. And Holmes' greatest enemy is not really Moriarty; it's himself, who risks his life to escape boredom and cannot pass up a puzzle, even the ones that might kill him. Episode one has a more complex ending as Moriarty and Mycroft are both busy scheming – though the killer is dead, the story arc is only beginning.

Canon References

- Since the Mycroft subplot didn't appear in the pilot, an e-mail to "mycroft@dsux.gov" is intended to cover his existence. The email reads, "When you have eliminated the impossible whatever remains must be the truth" from "The Sign of Four" and famous from the Holmes canon.
- In both this and the original novel, Mike Stamford and Watson have a meal in the Criterion Bar (which the creators had trouble rebooking). In the first episode, they get Criterion takeout coffee.
- Sherlock's emails in the pilot read:

  smith@smithson.org: The curious cow

  This is likely a reference to "The Adventure of the Priory School," involving strange cow tracks (though the famous line of "the curious incident of the dog in the night time" from "Silver Blaze" also seems possible).

  jones@jkjoes.com: Samson and Del

  This is less clear, though "The Crooked Man" references the similar Bible lesson of David and Bathsheba. Jones is a canon detective.

  drhopps@drdoc.net: Strange substance in pocket

  This could be anything – most original cases feature men with odd items in their pockets.

  gregson@ftnu.co.uk: RE: Church bell theft "Davies is your man"

The 1944 movie, *The Scarlet Claw* (often considered one of the best) begins with an ominous echo of church bells. Church bells are also heard in "The Naval Treaty" "The Adventure of the Bruce-Partington Plans," and "The Adventure of Black Peter"…if the church bell is stolen, there will be less drama in Sherlock's classic adventures. This could also be a nod to Dr. Joseph Bell, Doyle's inspiration for Sherlock Holmes.

Another intriguing possible reference is to *Doctor Who*, written by Gatiss, Moffat, and Davies – "The Lazarus Experiment" stars Gatiss as a monster defeated by church bells. It must also be noted that "The Adventure of the Tolling Bell" was a case in Basil Rathbone's *New Adventures of Sherlock Holmes* radio show. Gregson is a canon detective.

- "Mrs. Hudson's Snax 'n' Sarnies" is a restaurant next door to 221B Baker Street – apparently she's meant to be a cafe owner. In the first episode, it's been changed into the real-life Speedy's Sandwich Bar

- While making the pilot, Moffat and Gatiss were having conversations about whether Sherlock was likeable. Gatiss notes: "Happily we were able to go "House"! Not because we played Bingo but because we could cite the wonderful precedent of a show clearly based on Sherlock Holmes with a very, very grumpy protagonist whom everybody adores." ("A Study in Pink" DVD Commentary)

- "Because the faculties become refined when you starve them. Why, surely, as a doctor, my dear Watson, you must admit that what your digestion gains in the way of blood supply is so much lost to the brain. I am a brain, Watson. The rest of me is a mere appendix. Therefore, it is the brain I must consider." This is original quote, which also appears in the pilot, reworked.

> SHERLOCK: You may as well eat. We might be waiting a long time.
> JOHN: Hmm. Are you going to?
> SHERLOCK: What day is it?

JOHN: It's Wednesday.
SHERLOCK: I'm okay for a bit.
JOHN: You haven't eaten today? For God's sake, you need to eat.
SHERLOCK: No, you need to eat. I need to think. The brain's what counts. Everything else is transport.
...
JOHN: So...you don't...do...anything. [presumably implying Sherlock is celibate]
SHERLOCK: Everything else is transport. [Nothing matters but his brain.]

Much of the original's story's beginning has Watson wondering at Holmes's profession.

MRS HUDSON: What about these suicides then, Sherlock? Thought that'd be right up your street. Been a fourth one now.
SHERLOCK: Yes, actually. Very much up my street.
JOHN (leaning forward in the chair): Can I just ask: what is your street?

Sherlock's contempt for the police is certainly canon.

JOHN (softly): What am I doing here?
SHERLOCK (softly): Helping me make a point.
JOHN (softly): I'm supposed to be helping you pay the rent.
SHERLOCK (softly): Yeah; this is more fun.
JOHN: Fun? There's a woman lying dead.
SHERLOCK: No, there are two women and three men lying dead. Keep talking and there'll be more.

Sherlock says: "Angelo, headless nun." Their catchphrase harkens back to an earlier, unexplained case that involved him appearing to throw a drunk Sherlock out of his café. "The Headless Monk" was a case in Basil Rathbone's *New Adventures of Sherlock Holmes* radio show of the 1940s. The headless nun, meanwhile, will reappear in "The Sign of Three."

Holmes's drug use is canon.

CABBIE: Do a lot of drugs, Sherlock 'olmes?
SHERLOCK: Not in a while.
CABBIE: I ask 'cause you're very resilient.
(Sherlock frowns in confusion.)
CABBIE: Most people would have passed out by now.
(Sherlock blinks, looks down, then reels away from the cab as he sees a hypodermic needle hanging from the underside of his left upper arm.
CABBIE: Course, maybe God just loves me.

His character from the book firmly believes God will force the guilty men he's executing to take the poisoned pill because God does indeed love him.

Watson identifies himself as Sherlock's doctor, something he also acts as in "The Dying Detective."

THE BLIND BANKER

The Title

Certainly, the banker's picture is blinded by the code. At the same time, the banker who is Sherlock's client is blind about what's going on under his nose and the talents of his old schoolmate.

The Story

A mysterious code is left as a warning and the men who see it are promptly murdered in their locked rooms. It's eventually revealed that museum restorer Soo Lin Yao, formerly involved with the Black Lotus Tong in China, is in danger as well. In the course of the adventure, her brother tracks her down with coded threats, then in person.

The gang with their incomprehensible yet publicly-displayed code that threatens its former member actually appears in many original mysteries: "The Boscombe Valley Mystery," "The Five Orange Pips," "The Adventure of the Dancing Men," "The Valley of Fear," "The Adventure of the Red Circle."

In "The Adventure of the Dancing Men," Holmes works out that there was a murderer (and thus the couple was not involved in a murder/suicide) because the husband shot his own gun out the window at the assailant. "The Valley of Fear" offers a similar book code.

"It is clearly a reference to the words in a page of some book. Until I am told which page and which book I am powerless." [...]
"Then why has he not indicated the book?"
"Your native shrewdness, my dear Watson, that innate cunning which is the delight of your friends, would surely prevent you from inclosing cipher and message in the same envelope. Should it miscarry, you are undone." ("The Valley of Fear")

In *The Blind Banker*, after Soo Lin reveals that the Tong use a book code, Sherlock and John have a similar conversation:

SHERLOCK: So the numbers are references.
JOHN: To books.
SHERLOCK: To specific pages, and specific words on those pages.
JOHN: Right, so, fifteen and one, that means...
SHERLOCK: Turn to page fifteen and it's the first word you read.
JOHN: Okay, so what's the message?
SHERLOCK: Depends on the book. That's the cunning of the book code.

In both stories, Sherlock realizes it's a book everyone would own, and tries several failed attempts. In the original, Watson suggests Bradshaw, a cartographer's book, but Holmes says the words inside wouldn't lend themselves to a code. It ends up being the Almanac. In the episode, it's updated to *London A to Z*, a map book that nonetheless uses the awkward street names to form its code.

In "The Valley of Fear," the gang's burn mark features prominently, marking members like the black lotus tattoo. Moriarty is the one to have aided the murderer into Britain, and this story features Holmes tracking the "spider in the web" and losing to Moriarty as the client is killed by his thugs.

Blog

Watson grows unusually introspective about the larger issue behind the detective work:

> I can't deny that I prefer this kind of life. Being a civilian doesn't suit me. But the thing is, this life we've chosen isn't safe. Sherlock chooses to be this crusading consulting detective and I choose to be his colleague. But he's becoming known. People know of him. It's like that taxi driver said about how this Moriarty knew about him. Then the opera singer, she knew all about him. How long before someone else comes after him? And what happens to the people like Sarah or Mrs Hudson when that happens? (Watson's Blog, "The Blind Banker")

Symbolism: Blindness

Almost the first image seen is a man blindfolded. In fact, characters not seeing the obvious (or not so obvious) is key in this episode. Sherlock can't see many facts about Watson – he misses Watson's attempt to ask for a loan, ignores Watson's photo of the crime scene, doesn't notice that Watson wants to be alone on his date. Soo Lin Yao begins to decode the syndicate's message, and Watson's date is the only one to notice she's written the code down. Shan, the Tong leader, makes equal mistakes, as she can't discover the thief, and mistakes Watson for Holmes (missing that his "I'm Sherlock Holmes!" speech was completely sarcastic). Detective Inspector Dimmock can't see Holmes's value…it's no accident Lestrade is absent on this one. Finally, the nine million dollar pin has been hiding in plain sight – even the audience's sight – from episode beginning. Most importantly, Holmes and Watson miss that Moriarty is behind the entire plot. They are indeed blinded, but enlightenment will come soon.

Canon References

🔺Other adaptors have combined stories to create a new adventure – *Murder at the Baskervilles* (1937) involves the kidnapping of Silver Blaze, for instance. *The Royal*

Scandal (2001) blends "A Scandal in Bohemia" and "The Adventure of the Bruce-Partington Plans."

- The Jaria Diamond mentioned at the beginning is probably the Mazarin Stone, since both stories feature attacks by thugs. In fact, in the original story, Holmes says, "No violence, gentlemen – no violence, I beg of you! Consider the furniture!" This time there's violence and the furniture is harmed.

- Holmes's college friend brings him a case – this happened in Holmes's early days of practice, as he notes, "Now and again cases came in my way, principally through the introduction of old fellow-students, for during my last years at the University there was a good deal of talk there about myself and my methods" ("The Musgrave Ritual"). Musgrave and the banker Sebastian are probably meant to be the same character. Doyle describes him: "He had changed little, was dressed like a young man of fashion – he was always a bit of a dandy – and preserved the same quiet, suave manner which had formerly distinguished him."

- Watson is often mistaken for Holmes, at least momentarily in the books.

- Sherlock says his solution is "only explanation of all the facts." He says this often in his investigations, noting, in one case, "The facts appear to admit of only one explanation" ("The Sign of Four").

- "I have no data yet. It is a capital mistake to theorize before one has data. Insensibly one begins to twist facts to suit theories, instead of theories to suit facts" ("A Scandal in Bohemia"). In this episode, Sherlock complains to Dimmock, "You've got a solution that you like, but you're choosing to ignore anything you see that doesn't comply with it."

- Locked room mysteries appear in "The Adventure of the Empty House" and "The Sign of Four," the latter of which has an acrobat climbing to upper floor rooms and the former of which has shots through the window. Both of these appear in the episode.

- Shaftesbury Avenue (location of the souvenir shop) appears briefly in "The Greek Interpreter," another story of a foreign woman in England and the brother who comes there seeking her.

- Holmes doesn't costume when begging to get into a flat, but he does shift his entire personality. "I may have remarked before that Holmes had, when he liked, a peculiarly ingratiating way with women, and that he very readily established terms of confidence with them" ("The Adventure of the Golden Pince-Nez").

- In the canon, Watson frequently leaves his medical practice in the hands of another doctor while he goes off to help Holmes on a case. In "The Blind Banker," John falls asleep in the clinic because he was helping Sherlock all night, and Sarah takes some of John's patients.

- Sherlock tells Molly, "Don't eat while I'm working. Digestion slows me down." In the books he has a similar quote: "At present I cannot spare energy and nerve force for digestion" ("The Adventure of the Norwood Builder").

- Holmes only wants to look at the dead men's feet in the morgue. Likewise, in "The Red-Headed League," he only wants to glance at criminal John Clay's knees.

- Antique Chinese pottery features in "The Case of the Illustrious Client."

- Sherlock mentions the worth of the hairpin is based on who once owned it. *Sherlock Holmes and the Deadly Necklace* (1962) features a necklace worn by Cleopatra.

- Sherlock is nearly killed by a dart, as in "The Sign of Four"

- Holmes battles with singlestick, mentioned among his skills in "A Study in Scarlet."

- Sherlock tells the policeman he's consulting with: "I have high hopes for you, Inspector. A glittering career." Oddly, Holmes does not say this in the books – he speaks of politicians' brilliant careers before some terrible scandal he must solve, and he once says of criminals, "If our ex-missionary friends escape the clutches of Lestrade, I shall expect to hear of some brilliant incidents in their future career." ("The Disappearance of Lady Frances Carfax"). Repeatedly, he establishes that the police will not have brilliant careers and are only adequate.

🐾 "I may tell you that Moriarty rules with a rod of iron over his people. His discipline is tremendous. There is only one punishment in his code. It is death" ("The Valley of Fear"). When Shan confesses she has failed and compromised them all, Moriarty has a deadly response.

Innuendo

> SHERLOCK: We're going out tonight.
> JOHN: I have a date tonight.
> SHERLOCK: What?
> JOHN: A date? It's two people who like each other go out and have fun.
> SHERLOCK: That's what I was suggesting.
> JOHN: No, it wasn't. At least, I hope not.

Sherlock ends up inviting himself along on the date and seems honestly surprised that John prefers the girl to solving crimes with him.

🐾 As a memory aid, Sherlock puts John's face in both hands, tells him to close his eyes, and then spins him round and round, making close eye contact. He seems to prefer doing this than hearing that Watson has the evidence on camera.

🐾 "Get a room!! Lol!!" says Harry Watson (Watson's Blog, "The Blind Banker).

Actor Allusions

🐾 Sherlock tries using Charles Darwin's *On The Origin of Species* to crack the book code – Cumberbatch played Joseph Hooker in the Darwin biopic *Creation*.

🐾 Sebastian Wilkes (Bertie Carvel) says he and Sherlock graduated from the same university. This actually happens in *Hawking*.

Pop Culture

🐾 "Over a couple days we'd encountered Chinese assassins, killer opera singers, secret codes, secret messages in the A-Z, smugglers and god knows what else. I'd even met a beautiful lady. It was all very James Bond" (Watson's Blog, "The Blind Banker). As John and Sherlock squabble on the blog, John suggests a Bond marathon. In fact, Roger Moore, a famous Bond, played the detective in *Sherlock Holmes in New York* (1976).

🐾 Dan Brown's novel *The Lost Symbol* appears among the books in flashback. Of course both this novel and the episode are about deciphering codes.

🐾 Sherlock and John are called to a meeting at Tower 42. This may be a *Hitchhiker's Guide* reference.

> SHERLOCK: Climbed up the side of the walls, ran along the roof, dropped in through this skylight.
> DIMMOCK: You're not serious! Like Spiderman!

SHERLOCK

THE GREAT GAME

The Title

The title of "The Great Game" may reference the "game" played by serious Sherlockian scholars who presume that Sherlock Holmes was a real person. It also emphasizes the fun Moriarty and Holmes are having while matching wits.

The Story

"The Great Game" is adapted straight from "The Adventure of the Bruce-Partington Plans" with a bit of "The Naval Treaty" and "The Final Problem" thrown in as well.

In "The Adventure of the Bruce-Partington Plans" Sherlock gets a surprising visit from Mycroft: government worker Cadogan West ran out on his fiancée late at night. He's later found with a smashed-in head on the train tracks, with some of the plans for the Bruce-Partington submarine in his pocket, and the rest of the plans have vanished. The solution of this and the television version are similar, with the young man's body placed on top of a train and tumbling off at the points. While the heroic Mr. West follows the traitor in the print version, the show incorporates some details from "The Naval Treaty" – as in this short story and the episode the greedy future brother-in-law Joe Harrison/Joseph Harrison has built up debts (stocks or drugs) and steals his future brother-in-law's technical documents. In this story, there's no murder – just an attempted one.

This of course is only one of several plots in "The Great Game," almost a background story to the foreground of Moriarty's schemes.

> "You haven't seen about Baker Street, then?"
> "Baker Street?"
> "They set fire to our rooms last night. No great harm was done." ("The Final Problem")

"The Great Game" begins with a similar explosion at Baker Street.

Following this, Sherlock must complete Moriarty's challenges: the swimming pool poisoning, the missing man, the dead celebrity, the art forgery, and finally Watson. There's a swimming pool poisoning in "The Adventure of the Lion's Mane," but this one actually is accidental. "The Boscombe Valley Mystery" features a criminal hiding in a foreign country. In "The Adventure of the Sussex Vampire," a bite appears to be injuring a child, but instead there's a poisoner about, using darts (analogous to the botox needles).

Blog

When Sherlock solves the first case, he sends a message to Moriarty by posting on his own website, "The Science of Deduction": "FOUND. Pair of trainers belonging to Carl Powers (1978-1989). Botulinum toxin still present. Apply 221b Baker St." Sherlock types other messages onto The Science of Deduction:

> Congratulations to Ian Monkford on his relocation to Columbia.
>
> Raoul de Santos, the house-boy, botox. (This sounds like Professor Plum in the Conservatory with the Lead Pipe)
>
> Found. The Bruce-Partington plans. Please collect. The Pool. Midnight.

Connie Prince's Blog offers messages as well:

> Kenny here. It is with the greatest sadness that I have to
> confirm that my dear sister departed this world yesterday.
> Her death has come as a great shock to us all. RIP sis xx

Sherlock has several posts where he challenges her fans in order
to get dirt on her life, as he describes doing in the episode.
Afterward, Watson posts:

> Sorry I haven't posted much recently. We've had a few
> cases which I'll write up when I get chance. Think I needed
> a break from it all really. That whole business in the
> swimming pool...I just needed to get away from guns and
> bombs and maniacs. Went to see an old mate in New
> Zealand for a couple of weeks. Sarah came too but we
> broke up shortly afterwards. Not sure my life with Sherlock
> is compatible with long-term relationships. (Watson's Blog,
> "Quick Update")

Symbolism: The Game

> SHERLOCK (walking back to the window and speaking
> softly, as if to himself): Oh. Elegant.
> (John raises his head and sighs in exasperation.)
> JOHN: "Elegant"?
> LESTRADE: But what was the point? Why would
> anyone do this?
> SHERLOCK: Oh – I can't be the only person in the world
> that gets bored.

It turns out Moriarty's first murder was Holmes's first case –
though they don't know it, they've been battling all their lives.
Moriarty's puzzles for Holmes are certainly set up like a game,
with time limits and penalties as both of them know the rules.
Moriarty makes a move, then Sherlock must make one and so
forth. Moriarty plays word games within games –   When
Sherlock requests time, he's given a countdown. Notably,
Moriarty plays a similar game in "A Study in Pink" – the bottles
contain lots of pills, four bystanders die, then the fifth murder is
meant for Sherlock.

The subtle message of this structure is that Moriarty and Sherlock are fundamentally enjoying their game – an activity traditionally done for pleasure as well as competition. "You're enjoying this, aren't you? Joining the...dots," Moriarty asks. This mirrors Professor Moriarty's remarks from "The Final Problem," as he tells Holmes, "It is necessary that you should withdraw. It has been an intellectual treat to me to see the way in which you have grappled with this affair..."

There's an enormous emphasis on the pleasure these men take in their puzzles – Holmes remarks constantly in the books that he values the puzzle for its own sake, and he ignores the check from "The Blind Banker." Moriarty too loves setting up elegant crimes and safeguards, far more than he loves the profit for them – as he remarks at story's end, he threw away a thirty million pound profit to play with Sherlock. Both seem relieved in "A Scandal in Belgravia" when they have an excuse to end their standoff and play again in the future.

> SHERLOCK: Carl Powers, killed twenty years ago. The bomber knew him; admitted that he knew him. The bomber's iPhone was in stationery from the Czech Republic. First hostage from Cornwall; the second from London; the third from Yorkshire, judging by her accent. What's he doing – working his way round the world? Showing off?

There may be a subtle message here: woman from the Czech Republic (letter), someone close to Holmes (swimming pool poisoning), all of England in danger (hostages throughout England), personal scandal in the life of someone famous (Connie Prince), fleeing the country with millions (Columbia), criminal from the Czech republic – if the clues are added up in order. And at the root of all this...a woman's phone.

Significantly, Moriarty says he doesn't need the Bruce-Parrington data. Presumably, he has a better way to destroy England using...someone from Bohemia. And he appears to be laying down clues to see if Sherlock will catch on. Of course, minutes after the events of this episode, Moriarty receives a call from femme fatale Irene Adler, who has all the tools in place to blackmail the British royal family along with a devastating fragment of message from Mycroft's secret project. She may already be Moriarty's partner and leaving calling cards about during "The Great Game," or Moriarty may be doing so himself. The Bohemian stationary addressed by a woman certainly supports the former. The term "Golem" is only significant for its country of origin but Connie *Prince* parallels the king of Bohemia as a clue for fans about what's coming next. Admittedly Irene Adler may only be associated with Bohemia in the fans' minds because of the original short story, but it still functions as a clue.

Canon References

- The Russian and his wife may nod to "The Adventure of the Golden Pince-Nez"
- In "The Final Problem," Holmes is just back from France and must face Moriarty. In this version, he's just back from Russia.
- The dressing gown is also taken from the books, as Holmes had an array of different dressing gowns. Mark Gatiss notes: "Eventually we went for this one – this blue silk one – but there will be more!" ("The Great Game" DVD Commentary)
- The scene of Mycroft's visit was cut down slightly. There was originally a reference to the Holmes boys' mutual strange childhood and the fact that Sherlock had rather spoiled the family atmosphere (with his father possibly having an affair and him revealing it) ("The Great Game" DVD Commentary). *The Seven Per-Cent Solution* (1976) is a movie about Sherlock's mother having an affair and the effect this had on his life.
- Mark Gatiss comments that years ago he wrote down a list of things he would love to include if he ever did a Sherlock Holmes story and one of the things was "221C" ("The Great Game" DVD Commentary).
- Holmes paints a smiley face using a can of the yellow spray paint from "The Blind Banker." Holmes then shoots repeatedly, tracing the smiley with bullets. This is

a nod to "The 'Gloria Scott'" where Sherlock shoots "V.R." (Victoria Regina) into the wall. As Watson describes it:

> I have always held, too, that pistol practice should be distinctly an open-air pastime; and when Holmes, in one of his queer humors, would sit in an arm-chair with his hair-trigger and a hundred Boxer cartridges, and proceed to adorn the opposite wall with a patriotic V. R. done in bullet-pocks, I felt strongly that neither the atmosphere nor the appearance of our room was improved by it. (The Musgrave Ritual)

SHERLOCK (swinging his legs around to the floor and sitting up to face John): Listen. (He points to his head with one finger.) This is my hard drive, and it only makes sense to put things in there that are useful...really useful.
(He grimaces.)
SHERLOCK: Ordinary people fill their heads with all kinds of rubbish, and that makes it hard to get at the stuff that matters. Do you see?
(John looks at him for a moment, trying to bite his lip but then can't contain himself.)
JOHN: But it's the solar system!
(Sherlock briefly buries his head in his hands.)
SHERLOCK: Oh, hell! What does that matter?!
(He looks at John in frustration.)
SHERLOCK: So we go round the Sun! If we went round the Moon, or round and round the garden like a teddy bear, it wouldn't make any difference. All that matters to me is the work. Without that, my brain rots.

"You see," he explained, "I consider that a man's brain originally is like a little empty attic, and you have to stock it with such furniture as you choose. A fool takes in all the lumber of every sort that he comes across, so that the knowledge which might be useful to him gets crowded out, or at best is jumbled up with a lot of other things so that he has a difficulty in laying his hands upon it. Now the skilful workman is very careful indeed as to what he takes into his brain-attic. He will have nothing but the tools which may help him in doing his work, but of these he has a large assortment, and all in the most perfect order. It is a mistake to think that that little room has elastic walls and can distend to any extent. Depend upon it there comes a time when for every addition of knowledge you forget something that you knew before. It is of the highest importance, therefore, not to have useless facts elbowing out the useful ones."

"But the Solar System!" I protested.

"What the deuce is it to me?" he interrupted impatiently; "you say that we go round the sun. If we went round the moon it would not make a pennyworth of difference to me or to my work." (A Study in Scarlet)

In fact, Watson manages to prove in this episode that knowing about celebrities, politics, and the solar system actually do matter to cases. By the end, they're watching trashy television together.

The stiff envelope Sherlock receives is on peculiar paper from Bohemia (now the Czech Republic but Sherlock keeps using the old name). This envelope also appears in "A Scandal in Bohemia" of course.

Sherlock makes a crack about Mycroft's diet. He's supposed to be fat in the books. Mycroft in turn is uninterested in going out and running the case, noting, "A case like this – it requires...(he grimaces in distaste)...legwork." He's famous for not wanting to do the investigative part:

"Possibly, Sherlock. But it is a question of getting details. Give me your details, and from an armchair I will return you an excellent expert opinion. But to run here and run there, to cross-question railway guards, and lie on my face with a lens to my eye – it is not my *métier*. No, you are the one man who can clear the matter up." ("The Adventure of the Bruce-Partington Plans")

- Sherlock's line, "I'd be lost without my blogger." is an update of his line in "A Scandal in Bohemia": "Not a bit, Doctor. Stay where you are. I am lost without my Boswell." This is historical figure James Boswell, a lawyer who was the great friend and biographer of Samuel Johnson.
- Sherlock comments disapprovingly on Watson's write-up of "A Study in Pink." Following this, he discovers that the police and Moriarty have been following it, and Moriarty sends him a lookalike pink phone.
- On the phone message is just the Greenwich Time Signal, also called the "Greenwich pips." Instead of five short pips and one longer tone, this recording has only four short pips and the longer one, indicating to Holmes both "five pips" and a countdown of five tasks Holmes notes, "Some secret societies used to send dried melon seeds, orange pips, things like that. Five pips. They're warning us it's gonna happen again." This warning system is central to "The Five Orange Pips." Gatiss notes, "The Doyle story of 'The Five Orange Pips' for example. The story wouldn't work today [it features the KKK], but the idea of getting those five orange pips through the post is wonderful, it's spooky" (Adams 4).
- In *Sherlock Holmes and the Secret Weapon* (1943) a message left for Holmes is really from Moriarty.
- *Sherlock Holmes and the House of Fear* (1945) sees men faking their deaths for the life insurance…until Holmes discovers their ploy.
- Sherlock's noting that Molly's put on weight from her "domestic bliss" is a direct update from his similar comment to Watson in "A Scandal in Bohemia."
- Jim's card identifies him as "Jim Zucco" of Dynamic Asteroid web design. George Zucco played Moriarty in the Rathbone films, a clue for

those watching with a microscope. In "The Valley of Fear," Moriarty is described as the author of *The Dynamics of an Asteroid.*

⛰In many stories, Holmes asks for Watson's impressions. Here, Watson tries it with the trainers.

> JOHN: How did I do?
> SHERLOCK: Well, John; really well.
> (He pauses momentarily.)
> SHERLOCK: I mean, you missed almost everything of importance, but, um, you know...

This mirrors text from a short story:

> "'Pon my word, Watson, you are coming along wonderfully. You have really done very well indeed. It is true that you have missed everything of importance, but you have hit upon the method, and you have a quick eye for colour." ("A Question of Identity")

> SHERLOCK: How quaint.
> JOHN: What is?
> SHERLOCK: You are. Queen and country.

Book Holmes, by contrast is patriotic, and in several cases saves Britain from foreign spies. Nonetheless, he notes in "The Adventure of the Bruce-Partington Plans" "I'm afraid," said Holmes, smiling, "that all the queen's horses and all the queen's men cannot avail in this matter."

⛰Sherlock notes, "All that matters to me is my work. Without it, my brain rots" compared with the original, "I cannot live without brain-work. What else is there to live for?" ("The Sign of Four"). In both stories, Sherlock comments on how hateful a peaceful, crime-free world is for him.

⛰The houseboy in "The Great Game" is the reverse of the one in "The Sign of Four" – His name is Raoul in the show and Lal Rao in the original book.

On the show, Sherlock adds, "I don't know what's got into the criminal classes." He says something similar in "The Adventure of the Bruce-Partington Plans":

> "The London criminal is certainly a dull fellow," said he in the querulous voice of the sportsman whose game has failed him. "Look out this window, Watson. See how the figures loom up, are dimly seen, and then blend once more into the cloudbank. The thief or the murderer could roam London on such a day as the tiger does the jungle, unseen until he pounces, and then evident only to his victim."

Lestrade asks, "You like the funny cases, don't you? The surprising ones?" Detectives in canon observe the same:

> "Ah, yes, that's another matter – a mere trifle, but the sort of thing you take an interest in – queer, you know, and what you might call freakish. It has nothing to do with the main fact – can't have, on the face of it." (Lestrade, "The Second Stain")

> Gregson rubbed his hands in a self-satisfied way. "I think we have done all that can be done," he answered; "it's a queer case though, and I knew your taste for such things." ("A Study in Scarlet")

221C looks like a murder scene's room described in "A Study in Scarlet":

> It was a large square room, looking all the larger from the absence of all furniture. A vulgar flaring paper adorned the walls, but it was blotched in places with mildew, and here and there great strips had become detached and hung down, exposing the yellow plaster beneath. Opposite the door was a showy fireplace, surmounted by a mantelpiece of imitation white marble. On one corner of this was stuck the stump of a red wax candle. The solitary window was so dirty that the light was hazy and

uncertain, giving a dull grey tinge to everything, which was intensified by the thick layer of dust which coated the whole apartment.

🔺Sherlock says, "The curtain rises" versus "Come, friend Watson, the curtain rings up for the last act" in "The Adventure of the Second Stain."

🔺Sherlock's cellphone list of the most wanted acts as his index of biographies.

🔺Dirt and pollen are "clear as a map reference to me" Sherlock says. Watson notes that Holmes has a practical knowledge of geology in "A Study in Scarlet," adding, "Tells at a glance different soils from each other. After walks has shown me splashes upon his trousers, and told me by their colour and consistence in what part of London he had received them."

🔺Sherlock notes, "People don't like telling you things – they love to contradict you" vs

"The main thing with people of that sort," said Holmes, as we sat in the sheets of the wherry, "is never to let them think that their information can be of the slightest importance to you. If you do, they will instantly shut up like an oyster. If you listen to them under protest, as it were, you are very likely to get what you want." ("Sign of the Four")

🔺Sherlock tells Watson, "get me data," something he says often in the series.

🔺John discovers that Sherlock was only pretending to let him do his own investigation while secretly following and observing. Holmes did this in several of Doyle's stories, including "The Solitary Cyclist," "The Hound of the Baskervilles," and "The Adventure of the Retired Colourman."

🔺After meeting with John at the train tracks, Sherlock suggests that they need to do some burglary. In Doyle's stories, Holmes often breaks into places.

🔺Mycroft's texts continue through the episode. In "The Adventure of the Bruce-Partington Plans," he writes, "The Cabinet awaits your final report with the utmost anxiety. Urgent representations have arrived from the very highest quarter. The whole force of the State is at your back if you should need it." These sentiments are mirrored in his demands for attention.

🔺Sherlock inquires about a car and requests change in order to examine a man's neck and wallet. He uses similar stratagems in many cases, from a fake limp so he can demand to borrow a bicycle to a mistake that the suspect must correct in his own handwriting. Watson usually falls for this trick.

> LESTRADE: Any ideas?
> SHERLOCK: Seven...so far.
> LESTRADE: Seven?!

"Any ideas?" "Seven, so far..." Sherlock says in "The Adventure of the Copper Beeches."

🔺"You do *see*, you just don't *observe!*" Also said in "A Scandal in Bohemia," but delivered to Lestrade instead of Watson this time around.

🔺Sherlock uses the pompous word "Meretricious" in three original cases as well as in this episode.

🔺The Vauxhall Arches are featured in "The Sign of Four."

🔺Sherlock brings Watson's gun for him – Sherlock is always telling him to bring it in the books.

🔺Sherlock's stance during his fight with the Golem imitates Jeremy Brett's pose in fight scenes.

🔺Prague and the Golem may be a nod to "The Adventure of the Creeping Man."

> JIM: Is that British Army Browning L9A1 in your pocket...
> (Sherlock reaches down to his trouser pocket and removes a pistol from it.)
> JIM:...or are you just pleased to see me?

At possibly their first face to face meeting in the books, Moriarty likewise calls Holmes on weapon-carrying, noting, "It is a dangerous habit to finger loaded firearms in the pocket of one's dressing-gown."

- The hidden snipers working for Moriarty appear in "The Final Problem" and "The Empty House."
- The fact that Sherlock and Moriarty meet at a swimming pool may be a reference to their famous confrontation at the Reichenbach Falls in "The Final Problem."
- John says to Sherlock: "You, ripping my clothes off in a darkened swimming pool. People might talk." In *The Private Life of Sherlock Holmes* after Sherlock has implied that Watson is his lover, Watson is petrified at the concept of "talk."
- The final lines of the episode are straight from Holmes and Moriarty's confrontation in "The Final Problem":

> "All I have to say has already crossed your mind."
> "Then possibly my answer has crossed yours."

- Other episode lines parallel:

> JOHN: There were times I didn't even think you were human.
>
> WATSON: There is something positively inhuman about you sometimes. ("The Sign of Four")

- Mycroft mentions a knighthood to Sherlock – in "The Adventure of the Bruce-Partington Plans," Mycroft says, "No, you are the one man who can clear the matter up. If you have a fancy to see your name in the next honours list–"
- John's psychosomatic limp returns for a few seconds at the swimming pool.
- Moriarty's line to Sherlock near the end of "The Great Game": "I mean, I'm gonna kill you anyway, someday..." foreshadows the next season.

Locations

🔺The planetarium scene was filmed in Cardiff Museum, the lab scene at Cardiff University.

🔺The young man with the bomb is in the middle of Piccadilly Circus.

🔺The pool is in Bedminster in Bristol. Mark Gatiss used to live there and swim in the pool. He notes, "And if anyone had ever told me that one day I'd be making Sherlock Holmes in that pool, I would have said, '...You have come from the future'." ("The Great Game" DVD Commentary)

Innuendo

> I could see the look in Sherlock's eyes - a flash of, not anger, but hurt. For a second, he looked like a little, lost child. I should have been horrified that he'd even doubt me for a second but, to be honest, it was so refreshingly human of him. He actually did value our friendship. He did, despite himself, care. (John's Blog, "The Great Game")

There's a famous moment in the books when Holmes shows his affection, in "The Adventure of the Three Garridebs":

> It was worth a wound – it was worth many wounds – to know the depth of loyalty and love which lay behind that cold mask. The clear, hard eyes were dimmed for a moment, and the firm lips were shaking. For the one and only time I caught a glimpse of a great heart as well as of a great brain. All my years of humble but single-minded service culminated in that moment of revelation.

> JOHN: (after Sherlock strips off John's bomb-rigged jacket and throws it away) I'm glad no one saw that.
> SHERLOCK: Hm?
> JOHN: You, ripping my clothes off in a darkened swimming pool. People might talk.
> SHERLOCK: People do little else.

> MORIARTY: I'll burn the heart out of you.

SHERLOCK: I have been reliably informed that I don't have one.
MORIARTY: But we both know that is not quite true.
Sherlock glances at John.

Actor Allusions

🔺 John spends an early scene in this episode wearing a bathrobe with a towel slung over one shoulder. *Hitchhiker's Guide*, once again.

🔺 In John's blog, he explains he was busy "visiting a mate in New Zealand." He was in fact filming *The Hobbit* there, with his friend Sherlock.

🔺 The photos of a young Carl Powers are actually childhood pictures of the show's Second Assistant. ("The Great Game" DVD Commentary)

🔺 The voice of the little boy is provided by Louis Moffat, son of Steven Moffat and Sue Vertue. ("The Great Game" DVD Commentary)

British Culture

At the end of "The Great Game," Sherlock sarcastically notes that Moriarty is a consultant criminal, called in so "Jim'll fix it." "Dear Jim, help me," he smirks. *Jim'll Fix It* was a popular show on the BBC from 1975 to 1994 hosted by Jimmy Savile. People – mostly children – would write to the show and would always begin their letter, "Dear Jim, please could you fix it for me to..."

> GATISS: Have you done *Top Gear?*
> CUMBERBATCH: No.
> GATISS: It's only a matter of time!
> FREEMAN: It's minutes away!
> GATISS: It is now!
> CUMBERBATCH: The track's waiting for me.
> GATISS: Sherlock on his bike; Sherlock in his funny car...
> FREEMAN: Sherlock on his penny-farthing.
> CUMBERBATCH: Sherlock in his horse-drawn cart.
> GATISS: Sherlock on *Total Wipeout*. It's only a matter of time!
> CUMBERBATCH: No! Oh, God! Imagine! ("The Great Game" DVD Commentary)

Doctor Who

"Don't make me order you." "I'd like to see you try," Mycroft and Sherlock say. The same lines appear in the *Doctor Who* episode "The Green Death" between Brigadier Alastair Gordon Lethbridge-Stewart (who works for the government) and the Doctor (who is an independent consultant).

A SCANDAL IN BELGRAVIA

The Title

"A Scandal in Belgravia" is clearly an update of "A Scandal in Bohemia," with a touch of "The Illustrious Client" thrown in. Belgravia is a fabulously wealthy district of London that borders Buckingham Palace. The story was changed from Bohemia because, well, why bother with the nonexistent Germany royalty when one can play with a far more British scandal in this London story?

The Story

In "The Illustrious Client," a young female person is in danger of wedding a heartless seducer. Sherlock is engaged by an officious man acting on behalf of royalty (it's heavily implied to be Edward, Prince of Wales):

> Holmes: "I did not understand that you were an intermediary. Who's the principal?"
> Damery: "Mr. Holmes, I must beg you not to press that question. It is important that I should be able to assure him that his honoured name has been in no way dragged into the matter. His motives are, to the last degree, honourable and chivalrous, but he prefers to remain unknown. I need not say that your fees will be assured and that you will be given a perfectly free hand. Surely the actual name of your client is immaterial?"

63

Holmes: "I am sorry. I am accustomed to have mystery at one end of my cases, but to have it at both ends is too confusing. I fear, Sir James, that I must decline to act."

Echoing this is Sherlock's line: "Mycroft, I don't do anonymous clients. I am used to mystery at one end of my cases, both ends is too much work. Good morning." In both versions, he refuses, but finally takes the case. Moriarty and Mycroft do not appear in the short story, of course.

Irene Adler in the short story is far from a dominatrix. As Holmes describes her, "Oh, she has turned all the men's heads down in that part. She is the daintiest thing under a bonnet on this planet. So say the Serpentine-mews, to a man. She lives quietly, sings at concerts, drives out at five every day, and returns at seven sharp for dinner. Seldom goes out at other times, except when she sings" ("A Scandal in Bohemia"). True she's an actress and singer, who roams the streets disguised in men's clothes, but she enters a conventional marriage in the middle of the story. Even her inappropriate relationship with the King of Bohemia seems to have involved a proposal and not necessarily an affair.

On the show, Holmes says he's never heard of her. In the story, he must look her up:

> "Kindly look her up in my index, Doctor," murmured Holmes without opening his eyes. For many years he had adopted a system of docketing all paragraphs concerning men and things, so that it was difficult to name a subject or a person on which he could not at once furnish information. In this case I found her biography sandwiched in between that of a Hebrew rabbi and that of a staff-commander who had written a monograph upon the deep-sea fishes.
> "Let me see!" said Holmes. "Hum! Born in New Jersey in the year 1858. Contralto – hum! La Scala, hum! Prima donna Imperial Opera of Warsaw – yes! Retired from operatic stage – ha! Living in London – quite so! Your Majesty, as I understand, became entangled with this young person, wrote her some compromising letters, and is now desirous of getting those letters back." ("A Scandal in Bohemia")

In both stories, Holmes decides that having them both in the photograph together is the terrible indiscretion and he suggests buying the photograph outright. When Irene Adler won't sell, in both versions, he dresses as a kindly clergyman, appears to have a head injury so he'll be invited in, has Watson fake a fire, and observes Adler's hidden cabinet.

> "When a woman thinks that her house is on fire, her instinct is at once to rush to the thing which she values most. It is a perfectly overpowering impulse, and I have more than once taken advantage of it. In the case of the Darlington Substitution Scandal it was of use to me, and also in the Arnsworth Castle business. A married woman grabs at her baby; an unmarried one reaches for her jewel-box. Now it was clear to me that our lady of to-day had nothing in the house more precious to her than what we are in quest of. She would rush to secure it." ("A Scandal in Bohemia")

On the show, Holmes quips that he hopes the locked safe doesn't actually have a baby in it. This speech is obviously condescending, as Holmes labels women as governed by instinct, not men. However, Adler realizes she's done this, in both versions. In the short story, she switches the photo for one of herself before Holmes can return.

Modern Irene texts him, "I saw you in the street today. You didn't see me," which fits well into the short story. While groping for his keys, a "slim youth in an ulster" slips past and says "Good-night, Mister Sherlock Holmes." ("A Scandal in Bohemia"). This line and the similar "Goodbye, Mr. Sherlock Holmes" appear multiple times in the show. With this farewell, Irene escapes safely with her new husband and lives happily thereafter.

Her all-important letter to him at the story's end is mirrored by the many texts the pair share onscreen. Her letter below is far more personal than their few short story scenes together – always retold after the fact, always with one or the other in disguise. Describing the most intimate scene of the show, alone in Sherlock's room, Mark Gatiss explains: "It's intellectual flirting, 'cause he thinks he's just trumped her there and she's trumped him." (Commentary, "A Scandal in Belgravia"). This letter from the short story has a similar tang:

"MY DEAR MR. SHERLOCK HOLMES, – You really did it very well. You took me in completely. Until after the alarm of fire, I had not a suspicion. But then, when I found how I had betrayed myself, I began to think. I had been warned against you months ago. I had been told that, if the King employed an agent, it would certainly be you. And your address had been given me. Yet, with all this, you made me reveal what you wanted to know. Even after I became suspicious, I found it hard to think evil of such a dear, kind old clergyman. But, you know, I have been trained as an actress myself. Male costume is nothing new to me. I often take advantage of the freedom which it gives. I sent John, the coachman, to watch you, ran upstairs, got into my walking clothes, as I call them, and came down just as you departed.

"Well, I followed you to your door, and so made sure that I was really an object of interest to the celebrated Mr. Sherlock Holmes. Then I, rather imprudently, wished you good-night, and started for the Temple to see my husband.

"We both thought the best resource was flight, when pursued by so formidable an antagonist; so you will find the nest empty when you call to-morrow. As to the photograph, your client may rest in peace. I love and am loved by a better man than he. The King may do what he will without hindrance from one whom he has cruelly wronged. I keep it only to safeguard myself, and to preserve a weapon which will always secure me from any steps which he might take in the future. I leave a photograph which he might care to possess; and I remain, dear Mr. Sherlock Holmes,

"Very truly yours,
"IRENE NORTON, née ADLER."

The original Holmes appears chagrined at being beaten, and never appeared to have a romantic attachment – only an intellectual respect. However, he refuses the king's emerald ring in favor of Irene's photograph – a marked display of sentiment. Watson concludes:

> And that was how a great scandal threatened to affect the kingdom of Bohemia, and how the best plans of Mr. Sherlock Holmes were beaten by a woman's wit. He used to make merry over the cleverness of women, but I have not heard him do it of late. And when he speaks of Irene Adler, or when he refers to her photograph, it is always under the honourable title of *the* woman.

On the show, Sherlock tells her, "Oh, enjoying the thrill of the chase is fine, craving the distraction of the game – I sympathize entirely – but sentiment? Sentiment is a chemical defect found in the losing side" ("A Scandal in Belgravia"). However, there may be far more underneath his words.

> JOHN: Why would he care? He despised her at the end. Won't even mention her by name – just "The Woman."
> MYCROFT: Is that loathing, or a salute? One of a kind; the one woman who matters. ("A Scandal in Belgravia")

Modern Holmes requests Irene's phone and even says please...though it presumably is useful as more than a souvenir.

> To Sherlock Holmes she is always THE woman. I have seldom heard him mention her under any other name. In his eyes she eclipses and predominates the whole of her sex. It was not that he felt any emotion akin to love for Irene Adler. All emotions, and that one particularly, were abhorrent to his cold, precise but admirably balanced mind. He was, I take it, the most perfect reasoning and observing machine that the world has seen, but as a lover he would have placed himself in a false position. He never spoke of the softer passions, save with a gibe and a sneer. They were admirable things for the observer – excellent for drawing the veil from men's motives and actions. But for the trained reasoner to admit such intrusions into his own delicate and finely adjusted temperament was to introduce a distracting factor which might throw a doubt upon all his mental results. Grit in a sensitive instrument, or a crack in one of his own high-power lenses, would not be more disturbing than a strong emotion in a nature such as his. And yet there was but one woman to him, and that woman was the late Irene Adler, of dubious and questionable memory. ("A Scandal in Bohemia")

Symbolism: Disguise and Costume

Sherlock begins the story by donning the iconic Holmes hat – ironically, he does it so he won't be noticed, but he becomes known for the hat in every subsequent episode. Obviously this is a mythology gag – such a hat is only known today for its Holmes association, and when Sherlock wears it, he soon becomes known as the hat detective – his fans begin to believe he always wears it. Afterwards, fans like the one in "The Reichenbach Fall" wear the hat to associate with him: "This isn't a deerstalker any more, it's a Sherlock Holmes hat," he complains.

Sherlock is actually naked about as much as Irene is, with the one addition of a sheet. His scene is mostly based in stubbornness – the more he's ordered to dress, the more he refuses. Royalty will not intimidate the master detective, and nor will his older brother. Of course, this episode may be Sherlock's first romance, and he struggles to decide how much to reveal, how vulnerable to make himself. The sheet is a good metaphor for this.

Meanwhile, Sherlock and Irene both begin costuming for their first meeting. Irene opens an entire wardrobe that functions like an arsenal for her – all her tools of seduction. Ironically, when she's naked, she's the most protected of all, as she calls it her "battle armor." It's Holmes and Watson who are intimidated by her state.

> IRENE: D'you know the big problem with a disguise, Mr. Holmes? However hard you try, it's always a self-portrait.
> SHERLOCK: You think I'm a vicar with a bleeding face?
> IRENE: No, I think you're damaged, delusional and believe in a higher power. In your case, it's yourself.
> ...
> JOHN: Could you put something on, please? Er, anything at all. (He looks down at what he's holding.) A napkin.
> IRENE: Why? Are you feeling exposed?

Irene makes astute, valid points about clothing and its meaning.

Sherlock puts his coat on her, and she instantly turns businesslike, asking him about the hiker with the bashed-in head case. Likewise, in the scene where she returns it, she acts as detective and solves his mystery – becoming Sherlock while wearing his wardrobe.

Finally, Sherlock ends the episode by donning a disguise and saving her – he is not her executioner (as he's dressed) but her rescuer. The episode emphasizes their shifting roles as the leader and follower, attacker and defender, and finally winner and loser as they rise and fall.

Blog

> I can't say much about the actual case because of the Official Secrets Act but the country was nearly brought to its knees by one person - Irene Adler. She's now under a witness protection scheme so we'll not be seeing her again. And Sherlock seems fine with that.
> Of course, he isn't fine with it, not really. But he'll get there. (Watson's Blog, "The Woman")

This case is set apart as Watson names the post "The Woman" rather than its sensational case title.

Irene's Twitter feed exists (with only a few posts on it). This one nods to the events of the episode:

> The Whip Hand @TheWhipHand1 Jan 12
> @KateK Just let yourself in. Practically everyone does.

Canon References

🔍Holmes hides from photos in Robert Downey Jr.'s *Sherlock Holmes,* shielding his face just as he does here. WATSON: I like the hat. HOLMES: I just picked it up. (Robert Downey Jr.'s *Sherlock Holmes*).

🔍When Sherlock grabs the deerstalker, Watson also grabs a hat: a flat cap like the one Watson wears in Basil Rathbone's Sherlock Holmes adventures.

🔍There are title shoutouts like "The Geek Interpreter" (for "The Greek Interpreter"), "The

Speckled Blonde" (for "The Speckled Band") and "The Navel Treatment" (for "The Naval Treaty").

▲ Mark Gatiss explains: "The climax of episode 3 is on the top of Bart's Hospital and [the newspaper headline 'Refit for Historical Hospital'] was a sort of seeding for the idea that there was some building work going on, which actually didn't happen" (Commentary, "A Scandal in Belgravia"). It will be significant a few episodes later.

▲ 1895, the number of views the blog is stuck on, is the year *The Memoirs of Sherlock Holmes* was published. Its last story, "The Final Problem," takes place that year. Steven Moffat adds: "1895 – for those of you that don't know – is supposedly the year when Sherlock Holmes was at the peak of his game in the original stories, and there's a wee poem about it always being 1895 – so now he's got a blog that is always 1895!" (Commentary, "A Scandal in Belgravia")

▲ Sherlock's inability to tell John's girlfriends apart nods to the fans' confusion over Watson's many wives (possibly as many as three) in the original series. Sherlock appears to have a perfect memory for everything in the world but them, suggesting he's deliberately snubbing them.

▲ "Sherlock Holmes and I looked blankly at each other, and then burst simultaneously into an uncontrollable fit of laughter" ("The Sign of the Four"). The characters also do this at Buckingham Palace.

▲ "The old wheel turns, and the same spoke comes up. It's all been done before, and will be again." ("The Valley of Fear") echoes Sherlock's "The wheel turns. Nothing is ever new," discussing Coventry.

▲ The sheet Holmes wears is actually rather canon. "The Illustrious Client" begins with Holmes and Watson at a Turkish bath wrapped in sheets, before Holmes dresses and meets his client.

▲ When Mycroft walks in and tells Sherlock to get dressed for his client, Sherlock asks, "And my client is?" The man who walks in says, "Illustrious, to the extreme," nodding to "The Illustrious Client." Also, "The Illustrious Client's" identity is revealed through a coat of arms. Several are on the wall behind Mycroft in his office.

🐾 Mark Gatiss notes: "There's a little thing there, sadly not captured, when I make the note about James Moriarty: I wrote it on my cuff, which is something Sherlock does in the original stories and I thought, 'Maybe that's a family thing'. I brought my own propelling pencil!" (Commentary, "A Scandal in Belgravia").

🐾 A prospective client tells Sherlock, "She's not my real aunt. She's been replaced – I know she has. I know human ash." "The Disappearance of Lady Frances Carfax" and "The Adventure of Shoscombe Old Place" have parallels.

🐾 The businessman "prepared to offer any sum of money you care to mention for the recovery of these files" echoes "The Adventure of the Bruce-Partington Plans" and "The Naval Treaty."

🐾 Holmes's two hundred and forty different types of tobacco ash are mentioned in the monograph he says he's written in "A Study in Scarlet": "'Upon the Distinction between the Ashes of the Various Tobaccoes.' In it I enumerate a hundred and forty forms of cigar-, cigarette-, and pipe-tobacco, with colored plates illustrating the difference in the ash." Perhaps Moffat assumed more cigarettes were available today.

> SHERLOCK: Precise details: in the last week, what's been cleaned?
> MRS HUDSON: Well, Tuesday I did your lino...
> SHERLOCK: No, in here, this room. This is where we'll find it – any break in the dust line. You can put back anything but dust. Dust is eloquent. (Fall)

🐾 In many adaptations, Holmes hates it when Mrs. Hudson dusts – in *The Private Life of Sherlock Holmes*, he

71

points out that the thickness of dust lets him calculate the age of the papers.

* "Any Ideas?" "Eight, so far." Compared with the text:

> "Do you see any clue?"
> "You have furnished me with seven, but, of course, I must test them before I can pronounce upon their value." ("The Naval Treaty")

* Holmes resents Watson publishing the unsolved cases on the blog. There are two short stories where Holmes is incorrect and others where his clients die.
* John identifies his middle name as "Hamish," from a popular fan theory.
* The thumbs in the fridge are from "The Engineer's Thumb," and emphasize Mrs. Hudson's often-grisly job. (It's odd that he'd keep them but the visitable Holmes museum on Baker Street in London has a thumb on the mantelpiece, just as oddly).
* Holmes announces the boomerang mystery is a six, and he doesn't leave the house for more than a seven. In the books, he and Watson run about the city with cane and service revolver, but it's suggested there are hundreds of duller cases Holmes solves at home (though he'd probably appreciate Wi-fi). In "A Study in Scarlet," he simply consults from the sitting room:

> "But do you mean to say," I said, "that without leaving your room you can unravel some knot which other men can make nothing of, although they have seen every detail for themselves?"
> "Quite so. I have a kind of intuition that way. Now and again a case turns up which is a little more complex. Then I have to bustle about and see things with my own eyes."

* The aluminum crutch in both the episode and "The Musgrave Ritual" is a quick mention of an unseen case.
* John questions why Mycroft doesn't trust his own Secret Service, to which Mycroft responds, "Naturally

not. They all spy on people for money." This nods to his bribing Watson in the first episode.

🔺Mycroft condescends to Sherlock about his case, something he does in the original adventures as well:

> SHERLOCK: I was in the middle of a case, Mycroft.
> MYCROFT: What, the hiker and the backfire? I glanced at the police report. Bit obvious, surely?
> SHERLOCK: Transparent.

> "By the way, Sherlock, I expected to see you round last week, to consult me over that Manor House case. I thought you might be a little out of your depth."
> "No, I solved it," said my friend, smiling.
> "It was Adams, of course."
> "Yes, it was Adams." (The Greek Interpreter)

🔺Since Holmes never mentions his mother in the books, it's possible his older brother was the caregiver. Or just bossy.

> MYCROFT: I'll be mother.
> SHERLOCK: And there is a whole childhood in a nutshell.

🔺 Watson's time in the Fifth Northumberland Fusiliers is mentioned.

> SHERLOCK: Why? You have a police force of sorts, even a marginally Secret Service. Why come to me?
> EQUERRY: People do come to you for help, don't they, Mr. Holmes?
> SHERLOCK: Not, to date, anyone with a Navy.

Though the government comes to him regarding the navy in "The Adventure of the Bruce-Partington Plans."

🔺Watson notes of Irene in Robert Downey Jr.'s *Sherlock Holmes,* "She loves an entrance." Walking in stark naked certainly counts. Irene Adler in this episode and in the movie uses nudity and a syringe of knockout drugs to get the better of Holmes. In both stories, she's also working for Moriarty, and he has the upper hand.

🏔️ Holmes emphasizes observing, not just seeing. Irene notes he was "very observant" of her measurements.

🏔️ "The Valley of Fear" also features a misidentified corpse with a destroyed face.

🏔️ Holmes and Irene have many scenes together, particularly in his flat – this is an enormous update from their momentary meetings in the short story. However, in the movie, *The Private Life of Sherlock Holmes*, Holmes must spend a great deal of time pretending to married to an ultimately treacherous female spy. She curls up in his bed, walks around naked, and flirts while in desperate trouble, much like Irene. Steven Moffat admits: "I suppose quite a lot of *Scandal* riffs on *The Private Life of Sherlock Holmes*" ("The Hounds of Baskerville" DVD Commentary).

🏔️ Holmes alludes to being rewarded with a knighthood. In the books, he declines one.

🏔️ "Vatican cameos" is used as a code phrase between Holmes and Watson – another nod to an unwritten case: "I had observed some newspaper comment at the time, but I was exceedingly preoccupied by that little affair of the Vatican cameos, and in my anxiety to oblige the Pope I lost touch with several interesting English cases" ("The Hound of the Baskervilles"). This was also made into a computer game in the eighties. Sherlock will use the phrase again at John's wedding.

🏔️ American trained killers appear in several stories, such as "The Valley of Fear" and "The Five Orange Pips"

🏔️ This episode contains a Christmas celebration – Watson and Holmes share a Christmas dinner at the end of "The Adventure of the Blue Carbuncle."

🏔️ In the books and on the show, Holmes plays popular songs and his original compositions on the violin. The latter help him think, but his friends prefer the former.

Holmes works out a mysterious number code, something he does in several stories. He adds, "Please don't feel obliged to tell me that was remarkable or amazing. John's expressed the same thought in every possible variant available to the English language." Watson certainly does in the books.

Moriarty texts "Jumbo Jet. Dear me, Mr Holmes, dear me." He sends Holmes this (without the Jumbo jet part) before murdering his client in "The Valley of Fear." This message, instead goes to Mycroft, the other Mr. Holmes.

Steven Moffat adds: "Also – and I'm just nicking this from Billy Wilder's film [*The Private Life of Sherlock Holmes*] – but you take John out of the equation and Sherlock is instantly more vulnerable. You're more fearful for him when he hasn't got his wing man." Thus Sherlock and Irene have many scenes without Watson, including their confrontation with Mycroft.

Sherlock goes abroad and saves Irene from death – the female's spy's adventures in foreign countries where she's finally sentenced to execution and Mycroft reports this fact appears in *The Private Life of Sherlock Holmes*.

In *Sherlock Holmes and the Leading Lady* (1991) an older Irene teases Holmes about naming her "The Woman" in Watson's story. She adds, "You and I…we should be above all pretense." She calls him Sherlock, unlike almost anyone else. In turn, Holmes is mostly cold, and ignores her advances as he pushes Irene to think and help him solve the case. Holmes wraps Irene in his coat as she starts to undress. Later, however, he warms to her and they nearly share a kiss. Much of this also appears in this episode.

Pop Culture

SHERLOCK: It's this, or *Cluedo*.
JOHN: Ah, no!
(He closes the laptop and gets up to put it back on the

table.)
JOHN: We are never playing that again!
SHERLOCK: Why not?
JOHN: Because it's not actually possible for the victim to have done it, Sherlock, that's why.
SHERLOCK: Well, it was the only possible solution.
JOHN (sitting down again): It's not in the rules.
SHERLOCK (furiously): Then the rules are wrong!

The *Cluedo* board appears to be attached to the wall by a knife, suggesting what happened the last time. In the U.S. the game is called *Clue*.

John's complex plan that Molly should get the cellphone from a safety-deposit box and then have one of the homeless network members bring it is reminiscent of the climax of *The Maltese Falcon*. Of course, Sherlock has it the whole time.

Innuendo

Irene looks at Sherlock's face and makes deductions as he does, though more emotional ones: "Hmm. Somebody loves you. If I had to punch that face, I'd avoid your teeth and nose too."

> JOHN: We are not a couple!
> IRENE: Yes you are.
> JOHN: Look, who knows about Sherlock Holmes, but for the record – if anyone still cares – I'm not actually gay.
> IRENE: Well I am. Look at us both.

Irene emphasizes that a person can want to date women and yet be consumed with caring about a man, sexual or not. John and Sherlock *are* basically a couple, in day to day interactions. Benedict Cumberbatch notes:

> "It says everything about their relationship. It says what the bond is and the care is, and it's everything that they don't say to each other but he's allowed to say, thinking that he's not there. That's where – as a romance – it's an incredibly British affair. There's an awful lot of beautifully understated

subtlety and nuance to it." (Commentary, "A Scandal in Belgravia")

🔺John has actually been counting Irene's 57 texts to Sherlock – jealous and uncharacteristic behavior.

🔺One of Irene's texts reads, "John's blog is HILARIOUS. I think he likes you more than I do."

🔺Sherlock insults John's girlfriends and can't manage to keep them straight. John abandons his dates to care for Sherlock, and he too confuses which girl is which – there clearly isn't much invested there. Jeanette points out that he's a great boyfriend...to Sherlock!

Actor Allusion

On the jet runway, the American agent calls Sherlock *sir* sarcastically. In the hit radio play *Cabin Pressure*, Cumberbatch is often treated to a similarly sarcastic "sir."

British References

The very old friend with several small dogs is presumably the queen of England. The "young female person" has a few options: Princesses Beatrice & Eugenie, Kate Middleton, Zara Phillips. Assuming Sherlock's world has the same royal family as ours does, of course.

Locations

🔺Mark Gatiss gave Production Designer Arwel Wyn Jones a list of things to appear in Sherlock's bedroom – the periodic table on the wall, with a scientific chart replacing typical people's art. There's a small picture of Edgar Allen Poe – as Sherlock Holmes was inspired by one of Poe's creations, C. Auguste Dupin. Moffat suggests that in this alternate universe, Poe would probably be the writer of the most famous detective. Above the bed are the rules of baritsu, the Japanese martial art that saves Holmes in "The Final Problem" (Commentary, A Scandal in Belgravia).

Buckingham Palace's exterior appears in "A Scandal in Belgravia" and "The Sign of Three." However, the drawing room where Sherlock Holmes nearly lost his bed sheet is actually Goldsmith's Hall in Foster Lane.

The exterior of Adler's house was 44 Eaton Square.

The exterior of the Diogenes Club is actually The British Academy at 10 Carlton House Terrace, right next to the Duke of York Memorial.

Battersea Power Station A is used for John and Irene's confrontation.

> MARK GATISS: Also a real privilege to film in Battersea Power Station. This room is in Monty Python's Meaning of Life.
> SUE VERTUE: And The King's Speech.
> BENEDICT CUMBERBATCH: Was it in Brazil as well?
> MARK GATISS: I think it might be, yeah.
> (Commentary, "A Scandal in Belgravia")

THE HOUNDS OF BASKERVILLE

The Title

Adapting this from "The Hound of the Baskervilles" is very little change in title, admittedly. This is the most adapted, possibly most famous, of the Holmes stories, and the creators wanted to keep the gothic ghost story elements.

> GATISS: It's the most filmed; it's the one that everyone knows – I think – the best, and therefore I felt more of an obligation to include certain things.
> MOFFAT: There are so many huge iconic moments that people expect: there's a dog, there's fog, there's Dartmoor – the stuff you'd better deliver. ("Series 2 DVD extra: 'Sherlock Uncovered'")

At the same time, there's a subtle clue – there are in fact multiple Hounds: the project, the live dog, and the hallucinations, as well as a human criminal.

The Story

"The Hound of the Baskervilles" begins with the ancient legend of Dartmoor – the hound of hell that carried off the wicked Sir Hugo. On the show, it's updated to an urban legend of genetic experiments and cloning from the fifties. Both stories offer the creepy Doctor Stapleton, who experiments with animals, or in the book, is a "naturalist" who collects butterflies and preserves them in his lab. There's also Mr. Barrymore, with a full black beard.

Both have the wealthy young Henry in danger – Sir Henry Baskerville or the aptly named Henry Knight. The latter's father was killed twenty years earlier; Sir Henry has inherited the Baskerville estate on the death of his uncle, apparently killed by the hound. Mark Gatiss notes: "Again it's about the modern equivalents. In the original, Doctor Mortimer comes and he says, 'I've got this legend to tell you,' and in most adaptations that's how it usually starts with Sir Hugo Baskerville...so we get the equivalent sort of thing which is to tell the bulk of the story by means of a living TV documentary" ("The Hounds of Baskerville" DVD commentary).

Both stories share a dramatic line – "Mr. Holmes it was the footprints of a gigantic hound." It ends a chapter in the book and Holmes makes Henry Knight repeat it on the show. Holmes seizes on the case because the word "hound is archaic and odd." Of course, in Doyle's time, it was not – the word is used over a hundred times throughout the series for all sorts of dogs.

The deadly Grimpen Mire, in which one step can kill someone, is updated to the similarly treacherous Grimpen minefield. Doctor James Mortimer is transformed to Doctor Louise Mortimer, psychiatrist – both are the close confidant of Henry.

Fletcher, the tour guide, says creepily, "Stay away from the moor at night if you value your lives!" In the book, a similar warning, cut from newspapers, arrives at Sir Henry's door before they leave, and the warning is repeated several times. In both stories, there's a giant dog footprint. The dark, misty moor is a place of terror, and Henry is attacked when he goes there. Nonetheless, Holmes uses him as bait to draw out the monster.

In both, the monster is an enormous hound, glowing, with enormous teeth and red eyes.

> JOHN: But that wasn't what you saw. That wasn't just an ordinary dog.
> SHERLOCK: No. (His gaze become distant.) It was immense, had burning red eyes and it was glowing, John. Its whole body was glowing.

In the book, the evil Stapleton buys a monstrous dog and keeps it in a mineshaft. He smears it with glowing phosphorus and sets it on Sir Henry. On the show, this is alluded to with the dog the B&B couple get. They likewise buy it to capitalize on the legend and they keep it in a mineshaft, but it's savage.

Of course, on the show, the dog is a hallucination (mostly), the fog is causing it, and Dartmoor holds a secret laboratory – all is different, but it's still a gothic thriller.

Lestrade visits "on holiday," as he says and adds in the episode: "I'm enjoying this! It's nice to get London out of your lungs!" In "The Hound of the Baskervilles" Holmes summons Lestrade and tells him, "I think we might employ it in getting some dinner and then, Lestrade, we will take the London fog out of your throat by giving you a breath of the pure night air of Dartmoor." In both stories, Holmes tells Lestrade to get his gun. What follows is a battle on the dark misty moors as the men wait in a hollow and then fire shots at the actual dog.

On the show the mist is hallucinogenic; in the book, Holmes calls it "the one thing upon earth which could have disarranged my plans" as it will block him from seeing and killing the dog. When the creature finally arrives in the book, it's monstrous:

> A hound it was, an enormous coal-black hound, but not such a hound as mortal eyes have ever seen. Fire burst from its open mouth, its eyes glowed with a smouldering glare, its muzzle and hackles and dewlap were outlined in flickering flame. Never in the delirious dream of a disordered brain could anything more savage, more appalling, more hellish be conceived than that dark form and savage face which broke upon us out of the wall of fog.

On the show, the terror is not from its appearance but from the accompanying drugs. In the book, Stapleton is lost in the Grimpen mire and drowns, while the villain of the show runs into the Grimpen minefield and dies there.

Symbolism: Light

The first scene shows Henry Knight running through the gloomy moor, being chased. Afterwards, however, his terror appears in scenes of light – his documentary interview, his session with Doctor Mortimer in his brilliantly lit home, with lamps and windows at every inch.

Famously, this is Holmes's gothic adventure through haunted moors and an ancient mansion with a family secret. However, the darkness has faded. Instead, Holmes and Watson descend into the top secret weapons base that's brilliantly, terribly white. The ceilings glow with sharp overhead lighting. White labcoats and bunny suits make the humans seem part of their ultra-artificial environment.

When Watson sneaks in later, the place is a bit darker when deserted, but only a bit. He slips into the white lab and is caught off guard by a tremendous spotlight that seems to hit him straight in the face. The world around him goes overexposed – both whitest whites and echoing sound as Watson flinches in pain. As his security card refuses to work, the entire room seems to conspire against him with thrumming electronics. The world goes dark and Watson cowers in terror before the growls of the hound. His flashlight, occasionally shined right at the viewers' eyes, only makes the scene more terrifying. Watson is not in darkness, but a terrifying mixture of golden light and menacing shadow. Sherlock arrives and turns on the white lights of the lab – all is well. But in fact, Sherlock is the perpetrator of this scene, and his appearance, surrounded by white light suggests the same amoral experimentation seen from the scientists.

The final confrontation in the hollow sees thick white streaks of fog slicing the blackness. Like Watson's scene of terror, they're not in total darkness but a combination of dark and light, complete with the blinding white of flashlights. The fog is the menacing weapon of the amoral scientists here, harkening back to the blinding white lab.

By reversing typical colors of good and evil, the creators build a world of shifting morality – it is the people devoted to progress who are the force of violence in this episode.

Blog

"Obviously, as a doctor, I've seen the effects of a number of different drugs but this...I hadn't just seen the hound. I'd heard it. I'd felt it getting closer. I'd felt the fear inside me..." Watson writes, bringing the scene intimately to life (Watson's Blog, "The Hounds of Baskerville").

> Dear Sherlock Holmes. I can't find Bluebell anywhere. Please, please, please can you help? I like to look at your stories and the stories that John Watson has put on here. Is he a real Dr? I know that you try and help people and try to find things that have got lost. Bluebell is not a person so it might not seem important but she is very important. Not like a person but a rabbit. I don't know what happened but it was funny. Bluebell started to glow at night time. Like a fairy. I went down to the garden and locked her hutch for the night, but when I got there the next morning before went to school she had gone. The hutch was still shut and locked up. Please, please, please say you'll help me. Lots of love Kirsty Stapleton aged 8. (Holmes's Blog: "The Science of Deduction")

Canon References

🔺 Sherlock begins the story by walking in covered in blood with an enormous harpoon.

> SHERLOCK: Well, that was tedious.
> JOHN: You went on the Tube like that?!
> SHERLOCK (irritated): None of the cabs would take me.

"The Adventure of Black Peter" has a similar scene:

> He had gone out before breakfast, and I had sat down to mine, when he strode into the room, his hat upon his head and a huge barbed-headed spear tucked like an umbrella under his arm. "Good gracious, Holmes!" I cried. "You don't mean to say that you have been walking about London with that thing?"

"And what about 'The Adventure of Black Peter?' It's not a very good story, really, but it starts with Holmes coming in carrying a harpoon having spent the morning spearing pigs. Why not?" Gatiss comments (4).

In the original, Holmes cannot leave London so he sends Watson instead. On the show he *says* he'll do that, but then they both go. Gatiss adds:

> The other famous thing about the original story: because Doyle – although he brought him back – was sick of him, Sherlock Holmes disappears for the bulk of the story. He sends Doctor Watson down. Although he does actually go himself in secret, most of it is told by Doctor Watson. So it was a thing of having the fun of going through the process of saying, "Oh, I couldn't possibly go," and then saying, "I wouldn't miss this for the world!" So hopefully if you know the story, for a Sherlock Holmes fan it's like, "Oh, they're not gonna...oh, are they gonna not do it?" ("The Hounds of Baskerville" DVD commentary)

In the episode and in "The Adventure of the Blue Carbuncle," Holmes tells a man he has a bet with Watson in order to extract information.

Sherlock searches in a slipper for his secret supply of cigarettes, while he and Watson keep their tobacco in a Persian slipper on the mantelpiece in many short stories.

> SHERLOCK: Cigarettes! What have you done with them? Where are they?
> MRS HUDSON: You know you never let me touch your things!
> SHERLOCK: I need something stronger than tea. Seven per cent stronger.

Holmes' seven-percent solution of cocaine is seen in "The Sign of the Four" and famous in Holmes lore, as a movie title among other things.

At the episode beginning, Sherlock smells Mrs. Hudson's perfume and tells her he's written a blog of perfumes. This comes straight from "The Hound of the Baskervilles":

> In doing so I held it within a few inches of my eyes, and was conscious of a faint smell of the scent known as white jessamine. There are seventy-five perfumes, which it is very necessary that a criminal expert should be able to distinguish from each other, and cases have more than once within my own experience depended upon their prompt recognition.

🐾Mycroft *is* the British government, Holmes says.

> "You told me that he had some small office under the British government."
> Holmes chuckled. "I did not know you quite so well in those days. One has to be discreet when one talks of high matters of state. You are right in thinking that he under the British government. You would also be right in a sense if you said that occasionally he *is* the British government." ("The Adventure of the Bruce-Partington Plans")

🐾Holmes says in the original that the legend would be interesting only to a collector of fairytales, and on the show he's offered the case of the rabbit that glows "like a fairy."

🐾Sherlock's frustration at boredom is straight from canon:

> Your mind: it's so placid, straightforward, barely used. Mine's like an engine, racing out of control; a rocket tearing itself to pieces trapped on the launch pad. I need a case!

> My dear Watson, you know how bored I have been since we locked up Colonel Carruthers. My mind is like a racing engine, tearing itself to pieces because it is not connected up with the work for which it was built. ("The Adventure of Wisteria Lodge")

In the Holmes movie *The Scarlet Claw* (1944) a glowing ghost is blamed for various murders, but the culprit has been hiding in plain sight in the sleepy little village.

The little girl trying to hire Sherlock to find her missing pet rabbit Bluebell echoes "Silver Blaze," in which a client hires Holmes and Watson to find his missing racehorse. Both stories take place in Dartmoor.

Mr. Frankland is from the books, though he's not involved in the story. Mortimer mentions, "With the exception of Mr. Frankland, of Lafter Hall, and Mr. Stapleton, the naturalist, there are no other men of education within many miles."

Frankland mentions he enjoyed "A Study in Pink" and the "Aluminum Crutch" mystery.

In the story, a candle shines out on the moor to signal someone, but it's a red herring – the servants are signaling a convict brother-in-law to come get handouts. On the show, it's equally a red herring, with a couple jostling the car's headlights. In both, the man's name is Selden.

Hypnotism appears in *The Woman in Green* (1945), *The Seven Per-cent Solution* (1976), and *Sherlock Holmes and the Leading Lady* (1991), among others.

There's a small dog in both stories:

> "It may have been – yes, by Jove, it *is* a curly-haired spaniel."
> He had risen and paced the room as he spoke. Now he halted in the recess of the window. There was such a ring of conviction in his voice that I glanced up in surprise.
> "My dear fellow, how can you possibly be so sure of that?"
> "For the very simple reason that I see the dog himself on our very door-step, and there is the ring of its owner." ("The Hound of the Baskervilles")

> ...tiny little hairs all over the leg from where it gets a little bit too friendly, but no hairs above the knees, suggesting it's a small dog, probably a terrier. In fact it is – a West Highland terrier called

> Whisky. "How the hell do you know that, Sherlock?" 'Cause she was on the same train as us and I heard her calling its name and that's not cheating, that's listening. ("The Hounds of Baskerville")

🐾Stapleton in the books abuses his wife. Stapleton on the show killed her daughter's rabbit. Louise Mortimer (show) and Miss Stapleton (book) start to tell Watson more than they should, but then the villain stumbles in and provides a distraction.

🐾Said by Sherlock Holmes: "It is an old maxim of mine that when you have excluded the impossible, whatever remains, however improbable, must be the truth" ("The Sign of the Four"). And in *Hounds*: "Once you've ruled out the impossible, whatever remains – however improbable – must be true." This is babbled, as if it's a common saying of his. In the books, Holmes refers to this phrase several times.

🐾"You've never been the most luminous of people, but as a conductor of light you are unbeatable," Sherlock tells John. "Some people who aren't geniuses have an amazing ability to stimulate it in others."

> "Really, Watson, you excel yourself," said Holmes, pushing back his chair and lighting a cigarette. "I am bound to say that in all the accounts which you have been so good as to give of my own small achievements you have habitually underrated your own abilities. It may be that you are not yourself luminous, but you are a conductor of light. Some people without possessing genius have a remarkable power of stimulating it. I confess, my dear fellow, that I am very much in your debt." ("The Hound of the Baskervilles").

In both stories, he means that Watson's wrong guesses give him inspiration for right ones. In the show *House* (originally meant as a Holmes adaptation), this issue appears in most episodes, as House can only get the right answer if Wilson babbles off topic until some word or phrase randomly sparks something.

There are less deliberate allusions as well: Apparently Rupert Graves was tanned from filming *Death in Paradise* in Guadeloupe, so they wrote in the "brown as a nut" line, quoting "A Study in Scarlet."

When John is registering at the Cross Keys Inn and sees the receipt for meat, the actual name on the receipt is "Undershaw Meat Supplies." "Undershaw" was Doyle's home.

An airborne chemical that provokes terror and paranoid delusions features in "The Adventure of the Devil's Foot":

> I had hardly settled in my chair before I was conscious of a thick, musky odour, subtle and nauseous. At the very first whiff of it my brain and my imagination were beyond all control. A thick, black cloud swirled before my eyes, and my mind told me that in this cloud, unseen as yet, but about to spring out upon my appalled senses, lurked all that was vaguely horrible, all that was monstrous and inconceivably wicked in the universe. Vague shapes swirled and swam amid the dark cloudbank, each a menace and a warning of something coming, the advent of some unspeakable dweller upon the threshold, whose very shadow would blast my soul. A freezing horror took possession of me. I felt that my hair was rising, that my eyes were protruding, that my mouth was opened, and my tongue like leather. The turmoil within my brain was such that something must surely snap.

Holmes and Watson react similarly to the drug of the episode:

> SHERLOCK: Always been able to keep myself distant...(he takes another drink from the glass)...divorce myself from...feelings. But look, you see...(He holds up the glass and glares at his shaking hand.)...body's betraying me.

🐾"I don't have friends...just the one" is mirrored in canon: Watson asks, "Who could come to-night? Some friend of yours, perhaps?"

"Except yourself I have none," he answered. "I do not encourage visitors" ("The Five Orange Pips")

🐾Watson is furious that Holmes locked him in the lab and terrorized him with a hound's howls. Sherlock retorts with "I had to. It was an experiment" and "It was all totally scientific, laboratory conditions – well, literally." Stamford introduces Holmes and Watson with a warning about this sort of behavior:

> "It is not easy to express the inexpressible," he answered with a laugh. "Holmes is a little too scientific for my tastes – it approaches to cold-bloodedness. I could imagine his giving a friend a little pinch of the latest vegetable alkaloid [poison], not out of malevolence, you understand, but simply out of a spirit of inquiry in order to have an accurate idea of the effects. To do him justice, I think that he would take it himself with the same readiness. He appears to have a passion for definite and exact knowledge." ("A Study in Scarlet")

🐾Henry Knight is terribly damaged from the psychological traumas he's undergone. Sir Henry begins brave and impulsive like Watson, but after seeing the hound, he's more traumatized: "He tried to stagger to his feet; but he was still ghastly pale and trembling in every limb. We helped him to a rock, where he sat shivering with his face buried in his hands."

🐾The action takes place at Dewer's Hollow – Holmes and Watson hide in unnamed hollows several times in the book.

🐾This episode and Robert Downey Jr.'s *Sherlock Holmes* both involve Holmes discovering the rational truth behind the rumors of dark magic.

🐾Holmes quotes French briefly – he does this often in the books.

Innuendo

- When the gay couple in charge of the pub assume Sherlock and John are a couple, John has gotten sick of correcting people and no longer bothers.
- Sherlock and John's room apparently just has one bed.
- Watson's date, Louise Mortimer, leaves after he's called Sherlock's "PA. Live-in PA." Afterwards, Sherlock asks a bit hesitantly if Watson got anywhere with Doctor Mortimer. It's unusual that he asks about another person's romance.
- When John and Sherlock sit together in front of the fireplace, there is a heart-shaped decoration seen in the background right between them. Sherlock is terrified in this scene because for the first time, he's feeling emotions that mess with his cold, detached intellect. He tries to detach and gain control, even sending John away with the line "I don't have friends." By the next day, he relents and calls John his only friend, valuing their relationship even if it makes him vulnerable.

Actor Allusions

- Watson calls Holmes "Spock." In fact, Cumberbach starred in a *Star Trek* movie. Spock also said the "when you have eliminated the impossible" line during *Star Trek VI*. In turn, Leonard Nimoy [Spock] played Holmes on stage.
- During the "memory palace" scene, the word Ingolstadt pops up – it's a German city in *Frankenstein*. Benedict Cumberbatch alternated the roles of Victor and the Creature with Jonny Lee Miller (Sherlock Holmes in *Elementary*) in a stage version.
- Sue Vertue mentions that the drawing of the hound shown in the documentary was drawn by Steven's and her son..."and colored by me!" ("The Hounds of Baskerville" DVD Commentary)

▲Actor Russell Tovey [Henry Knight] is of course known from the modern/gothic series *Being Human*. Werewolves are an issue for him there as well.

Setting

▲ Grimpon village doesn't really exist, so the small Welsh village of St Hilary was used, along with establishing shots from Dartmoor.

▲ The exteriors of the Baskerville Research Facility are actually a Liquified Natural Gas [LNG] Storage Facility run by The Hardstaff Group.

▲ Three Bear's Cave in Forest Fawr Country Park, a former iron mine, is used for Dewer's Hollow.

Pop Culture

Mark Gatiss: "Oh yeah. This is a steal from *Jaws*. It's exposition done by a master. There's a scene in *Jaws* when Richard Dreyfuss and Roy Scheider are out with all this amazing equipment and he says, 'This is...are you...are you...rich?' 'Yeah.'" ("The Hounds of Baskerville" DVD Commentary)

Doctor Who

> MOFFAT: Almost more importantly than the modernising of Sherlock Holmes, he's still a young man; he's still forming. He's not the big monolithic Sherlock Holmes yet – he's still encountering Irene and wondering if actually that's what he should be doing, or actually facing the idea that he is capable of being tremendously frightened. I wouldn't believe this moment of a fifty year old Sherlock Holmes; I'd think, He would know, "Yes of course I can be frightened", but he's still on the training slopes, as it were.
> GATISS: It's an eternal problem, of course...It's a bit like the Doctor [in *Doctor Who*]. If you also accept his universal brilliance, then what's to stop him just shutting down the story? That's always a problem – especially with Sherlock Holmes because of his breadth of intelligence and

knowledge – is that he will just spoil it. ("The Hounds of Baskerville" DVD Commentary)

THE REICHENBACH FALL

The Title

The original story is "The Final Problem" (name-checked in the text). It involves Holmes meeting his death by falling into a chasm at Reichenbach Falls in Switzerland. This story of course puns on the "fall," as Sherlock is discredited as well as killed. Sherlock begins the tale as the hero of the *Falls of the Reichenbach*, Turner's masterpiece painting that's been recovered by the detective, and ends with his reputation and body broken...or at least someone's body.

The Story

As Sherlock tells the court, "James Moriarty isn't a man at all – he's a spider; a spider at the center of a web – a criminal web with a thousand threads and he knows precisely how each and every single one of them dances." This is of course from the book:

> He is the Napoleon of crime, Watson. He is the organizer of half that is evil and of nearly all that is undetected in this great city. He is a genius, a philosopher, an abstract thinker. He has a brain of the first order. He sits motionless, like a spider in the center of its web, but that web has a thousand radiations, and he knows well every quiver of each of them. He does little himself. He only plans. But his agents are numerous and splendidly organized. ("The Final Problem")

Both stories begin with Watson sadly putting his friend's fate into words. The short story begins with Moriarty setting assailants on Holmes after Holmes is drawing a trap around his great nemesis. The show has Moriarty waging colossal crimes. After Moriarty's spectacular break in and trial, the story's real conflict begins. He stops by Holmes' house for tea and a chat. The same happens in the short story – Holmes offers Moriarty a chair and they have a pleasant discussion, both acknowledging they're intellectual equals who understand all of each other's plans.

In the book, Moriarty's master plan and his mistake are hidden from Watson – the story is about him and Holmes fleeing the master criminal for their lives. They travel to Switzerland and visit the majestic Reichenbach Falls. There, Watson receives a message there's a dying English lady, just as on the show he gets a message that Mrs. Hudson has been shot. Both times, he hurries off and the great detective and criminal face off.

In both stories, Holmes takes a moment before his impending death to say a farewell to Watson; in both stories, Moriarty is completely willing to die in order to get his revenge. In the short story, Moriarty rushes at Holmes, and Watson arrives to see only two sets of tracks in the mud leading off the cliff to the stunning drop below. The Great Detective has died ridding the world of its greatest criminal.

Originally, Doyle intended to kill off his character – he relented after years of fannish pressure and brought him back in "The Empty House." Today's fans, of course, had less wait, as they were assured Sherlock would return.

Symbolism: Grimm's

Moriarty sits on a throne with crown and scepter, plays with an apple he offers Sherlock. When they meet at 221B, he takes a tea cup with a crown on it and boasts to Sherlock that "the man with the key is king." He is the ruler of his own story, and he sets up the entire plot as he notes, "every fairy tale needs a good old-fashioned villain." If he is the king and Sherlock as he calls him is Sir Boast-a-lot, then Sherlock will bring down the kingdom with his own selfishness as Lancelot does.

Most fairytales have events come in threes: three brothers, three trips to the ball or visits from the evil queen. Moriarty uses this number as well. He breaks into the three most secure places in the country. His message for Sherlock, I O U, consists of three letters. He leaves the message three times (on the apple, in front of the precinct and in a Graffiti close to Baker Street). He sends his three assassins to attack three victims: "Three bullets; three gunmen; three victims."

Moriarty uses old-fashioned wax seals for the envelope with the Grimm's Brothers collection, the burnt gingerbread man, and the breadcrumbs. At the same time, linseed oil and footprints make another kind of breadcrumbs...they're even left by the boy (Hansel) rather than the girl. The gingerbread man is a particular message, as in the story, all he does is run and run (though he's eaten nonetheless). Holmes, the gingerbread man, will be killed, while Hansel and Gretel are used to kill the villain – here Holmes must take the place of the witch and get pushed into the oven.

Snow White has interesting parallels with the tests Moriarty gives Sherlock, set off with his playing with an apple:

> If you look at the tale you realize that it basically contains all the "tests" Moriarty designed for Sherlock during the first season. Snow White flees into the forest while the hunter brings the Evil Queen "proof" of her death mirrors (no pun intended) Ian Monkford faking his death. The first murder attempt on Snow White is done with a laced bodice used to asphyxiate her, which is basically the murder method of the golem, minus the bodice, naturally. The second time the Evil Queen uses a poisoned comb, which is similar to kill Connie Prince by injecting poison into her head. The third time she uses an apple, of which one half is poisoned (which she gives Snow White) and the other one not (which she eats herself), a nod to the Jefferson Hopes killing method with the two pills. The tale ends with the Evil Queen dancing to death in fiery shoes, which was basically Carl Powers fate (and if you remember that part of the story, the quote "I like to watch you dance" becomes an even more sinister meaning). (SwanPride)

Finally, the deaths and near-deaths at the end are seen in Snow White and many other tales. When trying to get Sherlock to jump off the roof, Moriarty says, "I love newspapers. Fairy tales. And pretty Grimm ones, too." However, Moriarty is the villain of the piece, much as he may try to hide behind his persona of a children's entertainer. He dies, caught in his own scheme, and Sherlock returns from death. Often the hero, like Snow White or Red Riding Hood will vanish from the world for a time before returning in triumph...of course, this is exactly what happens in season three.

Blog

Conspicuously, there's no blog entry...Watson can't bear to write one.

Canon References

The Reichenbach Fall shows Holmes getting gifts like cufflinks and a tie. In the books, he also gets particular gifts:

> He held out his snuffbox of old gold, with a great amethyst in the centre of the lid. Its splendour was in such contrast to his homely ways and simple life that I could not help commenting upon it.
> "Ah," said he, "I forgot that I had not seen you for some weeks. It is a little souvenir from the King of Bohemia in return for my assistance in the case of the Irene Adler papers."
> "And the ring?" I asked, glancing at a remarkable brilliant which sparkled upon his finger.
> "It was from the reigning family of Holland, though the matter in which I served them was of such delicacy that I cannot confide it even to you, who have been good enough to chronicle one or two of my little problems." (A Case of Identity)

🔺A newspaper article reveals that Arthur Conan Doyle is a well-known writer in Sherlock's universe.

🔺Ricoletti of the club-foot and his abominable wife are a past case of Holmes's from the books. On television, Sherlock tracks down "Peter Ricoletti: number one on Interpol's Most Wanted list since nineteen eighty-two."

🔺In Rathbone's *The Adventures of Sherlock Holmes* (1939), Moriarty attempts to steal the crown jewels through distraction and misdirection.

🔺Sherlock visualizes a map of London and mentally visits possible locations, including Norwood, a reference to "The Adventure of the Norwood Builder."

🔺In "The Adventure of the Illustrious Client," a fierce young woman named Kitty Winter is determined to destroy the adored Baron Gruner's reputation. Reporter Kitty Riley destroys Sherlock's reputation in "The Reichenbach Fall." In both, Sherlock uses the newspapers as a tool to spread false information and win the day (a very subtle clue to his revelation in "The Empty Hearse").

🔺Holmes is investigating a faked suicide – another occurs in "The Resident Patient."

🔺Watson is horrified at being called "...confirmed bachelor John Watson." In the movie *The Private Life of Sherlock Holmes*, Holmes uses this term to imply he and Watson have a relationship, to get him out of a romantic entanglement. Watson is furious there as well.

🔺Moriarty taunts Holmes many times with the "final problem" – the title of the short story that mirrors this episode.

🔺Steven Moffat notes:

> There's a sequence where Moriarty arrives in Baker Street and we lifted it wholesale from an ancient Sherlock Holmes film called Woman in Green with Basil Rathbone, and it's a very very brilliant little sequence. Sherlock Holmes is upstairs playing the violin and Moriarty creeps from the

> shadows and he starts going up the stairs, and suddenly the violin stops, and then Moriarty stops too 'cause he realises he's been clocked. He waits for a second, then the violin starts again and then Moriarty continues the ascent. And it's all told in one shot; it tells you the whole story: the whole idea is [that] Sherlock knows that he's coming, he's cool with the fact he's coming, and Moriarty's cool with the fact that he knows he's coming. If that little sequence had appeared in a Hitchcock movie people would have written essays about it, but we've just taken that and borrowed it." ("The Hounds of Baskerville" DVD Commentary)

⚠ When Moriarty visits, Sherlock is playing Bach's Sonata No. 1 in G minor, and they have a conversation about the composer. Sherlock also plays Bach in *The Case of the Silk Stocking* (2004).

⚠ There's a bank robbery in "The Red-Headed League" of "one of the principal London banks" compared with the bank attack here.

⚠ "Everyone has a weak spot and he found mine," Irene Adler tells Holmes in Robert Downey Jr.'s *Sherlock Holmes*. This is Moriarty's method of operation in this episode.

⚠ In "A Study in Pink," the murderer notes no one ever pays attention to their cab driver. In this episode, Sherlock fails to notice his cab driver is Moriarty.

⚠ Watson asks all the members for help in the Diogenes Club – the ultimate no-no. As Sherlock explains in the books:

> "It now contains the most unsociable and unclubable men in town. No member is permitted to take the least notice of any other one. Save in the Stranger's Room, no talking is, under any circumstances, allowed, and three offences, if brought to the notice of the committee, render the talker liable to expulsion. My brother was one of the founders, and I have myself found it a very soothing atmosphere." ("The Greek Interpreter")

🔍 The old gentleman in the Diogenes Club is played by Douglas Wilmer who played the role of Sherlock Holmes in a BBC series in the 1960s.

🔍 Jeremy Brett's *Sherlock Holmes* series also has white shoe covers in the Diogenes Club.

🔍 Mycroft says they don't want a repeat of 1972...a movie of *Hound of the Baskervilles* came out that year.

🔍 *The Private Life of Sherlock Holmes* (1970) suggests the Diogenes Club is actually a front for the British Secret Service. Possible events in 1972 include The Battle of Mirbat or unrest in Northern Ireland. The climax of the fictional *Tinker Tailor Soldier Spy* takes place then as well.

🔍 The U.S. Ambassador's children are kidnapped from St Aldate's, a "Posh boarding place down in Surrey." Many of Holmes's cases take place in Surrey and there's a boarding school kidnapping in "The Adventure of the Priory School" (no fairytales or gingerbread, however).

🔍 Holmes's famous crime-solving methods involve analyzing footprints ("A Study in Scarlet," "The Boscombe Valley Mystery"), analyzing mud ("The Adventure of the Three Students"), and putting himself in the kidnapper's or victim's shoes – in "The Adventure of the Retired Colourman" like this one, Holmes guesses the victim wrote a note. Also in this case and in "The Sign of Four," the criminal steps in something smelly and leaves a trail.

🔍 Sherlock uses his homeless network again. They're a deliberate update to the Baker Street Irregulars, a gang of street kids Holmes would pay to spy on people and places.

🔍 As Holmes notes, "Rich Brook in German is Reichen Bach – the case that made my name." Moriarty is a full-time career criminal, but here claims to be an innocent actor for children. His book counterpart is a respected professor of mathematics. In *The Seven-Per-Cent Solution* (1976), Moriarty actually is a simple tutor, with his villainy a fantasy of Holmes's drug habit.

🔺In the short story, assassins attack Holmes; on the show, they're mysteriously trying to save him – both are at Moriarty's behest.

🔺In this episode and in Robert Downey Jr.'s *Sherlock Holmes*, Holmes is arrested by the police. In the movie, Holmes notes, "There was never any magic. Only conjuring tricks. The simplest involves paying people off. Like the prison guard who pretended to be possessed outside your cell. Your reputation and the inmates' fear did the rest. Others required more elaborate preparations." This is basically the truth behind Moriarty's magic code in this episode – it's a fraud but Moriarty's reputation and his paid allies pulled it off and made it look convincing. Likewise, the device everyone wants in the movie will allow the control of any device, much like the one Moriarty claims to have in this episode.

🔺*Sherlock Holmes and the Baker Street Irregulars* also sees Holmes arrested – the detectives assume he's behind the murder of police officers because he's jealous of them taking the credit. It seems someone else is actually jealous…

🔺*The Woman in Green* (1945) sees Moriarty forcing Holmes to write a suicide note then kill himself. If he does not, Watson will die. However, Holmes outwits him and Moriarty kills himself in the end.

🔺*Sherlock Holmes: A Game of Shadows* sees the double sacrifice at Reichenbach Falls specifically to protect Watson from being killed by Moriarty.

🔺 The following passages have interesting links to Sherlock's death scene: Watson gets a momentary feel of his friend's wrist, and then is dragged away:

> "But why would you not let me near you, since there was in truth no infection?"
> "Can you ask, my dear Watson? Do you imagine that I have no respect for your medical talents? Could I fancy that your astute judgment would pass a dying man who, however weak, had

no rise of pulse or temperature? At four yards, I could deceive you." ("The Dying Detective")

I am not a whole-souled admirer of womankind, as you are aware, Watson, but my experience of life has taught me that there are few wives having any regard for their husbands who would let any man's spoken word stand between them and that husband's dead body. Should I ever marry, Watson, I should hope to inspire my wife with some feeling which would prevent her from being walked off by a housekeeper when my corpse was lying within a few yards of her. ("The Valley of Fear")

- Moriarty's claim to be an actor hired by Holmes echoes *Without a Clue*, in which Watson, the real crime solver, hires an actor to be his Sherlock.
- At the beginning of "A Study in Scarlet," Watson writes "...be it remembered how objectless was my life and how little there was to engage my attention....and I had no friends who would call upon me and break the monotony of my daily existence." At the graveyard he voices similar sentiments.
- John's psychosomatic limp appears briefly as he walks away from Sherlock's grave.

Actor Allusions

In "The Reichenbach Fall," Sherlock tells Lestrade that "You can't kill an idea," though the latter man was trying to do so as a detective in *V for Vendetta*.

Pop Culture

MYCROFT: Too much history between us, John. Old scores; resentments.
JOHN: Nicked all his Smurfs? Broke his Action Man?

LESTRADE: Yeah, well, you know what he's like – CSI Baker Street

- Richard Brook's CV includes the clown Touchstone in *As You Like It* and Algy in *The Importance of Being Earnest*—both liars and deceivers. He plays Achilles (a dead hero and possible play on "Achilles heel") as well as Hamlet (also grandiose and dead) and Edmund, the dying young political rebel of *Long Day's Journey into Night*. This all appears to be foreshadowing, or a subtle threat against Sherlock.
- At Sherlock's grave, John calls him the "Most human human being that [he's] ever known." This echoes Captain Kirk's speech at Spock's funeral at the end of Wrath of Khan, saying that "of all the souls [he] have encountered in all of [his] travels, [Spock's] was the most human.

Setting

- The Old Bailey, officially known as the Central Criminal Court, is arguably the single most famous court in the world. The exteriors were used for filming (St. Bart's is opposite) while the court room itself was filmed in Swansea Guildhall, with Roath police station in Wales as the holding cells.
- John's final scene at the grave was filmed in St Woolos Cemetery in Newport in Wales. This was also used in Doctor Who, including for Moffat's episode "Blink."

Doctor Who

Watson begins the episode saying, "My best friend, Sherlock Holmes, is dead." This echoes Rose Tyler's "This is the story of how I died." Both begin in mourning, flash back through the story, then finally reveal the protagonist is still alive, just missing.

Innuendo

🔸John is horrified at being labeled "confirmed bachelor John Watson" and tells Sherlock, "Okay, this is too much. We need to be more careful."

🔸When the two are handcuffed together, they hold hands. John notes, "Now people will definitely talk," a nod to his earlier "I'm glad no one saw that. People might talk" in "The Great Game."

🔸When John returns to his therapist, John says there's something he wished he'd said but he can't voice it. At the graveside, John pleads for Sherlock to perform "one more miracle" and be alive for him.

🔸Kitty Riley shouts after Sherlock, "So, you and John Watson, just platonic? Shall I put you down for a no on that too –" and Sherlock returns to confront her.

🔸From Moriarty's first message to Sherlock, "Hello, Sexy!" he appears to be flirting, even though he claims to have been only playing gay during their first meeting as part of his disguise ("Did you like the little touch with the underwear?").

> MORIARTY: Is that a British Army Browning L9A1 in your pocket, or are you just pleased to see me?
> SHERLOCK: Both.
> (later)
> MORIARTY: But the flirting's over, Sherlock. (sing song) Daddy's had enoooough nooooow!
>
> SHERLOCK: We met twice, five minutes in total. I pulled a gun, he tried to blow me up. I felt we had a special something.
> (later)
> SHERLOCK: Unless I kill myself. Complete your story.
> MORIARTY: You gotta admit that's sexier.

John comments to Sherlock, "I'm sure you'll be very happy together."

SHERLOCK

MINI EPISODE: MANY HAPPY RETURNS

The Title

The phrase is equivalent to "Happy Birthday" and Lestrade delivers John's birthday message from Sherlock. Of course, there's a pun on "return." This small webisode, taking place just before the third series, is on BBC's You Tube Channel.

The Story

Holmes describes his three-year absence thus in "The Empty House":

> I travelled for two years in Tibet, therefore, and amused myself by visiting Lhassa and spending some days with the head Llama. You may have read of the remarkable explorations of a Norwegian named Sigerson, but I am sure that it never occurred to you that you were receiving news of your friend. I then passed through Persia, looked in at Mecca, and paid a short but interesting visit to the Khalifa at Khartoum, the results of which I have communicated to the Foreign Office. Returning to France I spent some months in a research into the coal-tar derivatives, which I conducted in a laboratory at Montpelier, in the South of France. ("The Empty House")

On the show, Holmes infiltrates "A breakaway sect of Buddhist warrior monks infiltrated by a blonde drug smuggler." From there, he travels to New Delhi, then Hamburg, then on to Amsterdam, and then Brussels. In both versions, his exploits become famous, but he is carefully not named, thus someone could follow his trail.

Blog

And now it's time for me to be honest. I'm meant to be keeping this blog to remind me of the good times. I know it's meant to be healthy but what's the point? I need to properly move on. I need to put it all behind me and move on.

And I'm so tired of deleting comments from people who don't believe me. Who think all this is a lie. I know it was real. There are so many people out there who know that all this was real. They believed in Sherlock.

And I've found someone. So I should concentrate on that.

So this'll be my last blog.

Sherlock, you bastard, wherever you are. Cheers.

Canon References

🔍Inspector Prakesh boasts, "After that it was simply a matter of tracking down the killer, which I did by working out the depth to which the chocolate Flake had sunk into the victim's ice-cream cone." This mirrors the short story line, "You will remember, Watson, how the dreadful business of the Abernetty family was first brought to my notice by the depth which the parsley had sunk into the butter upon a hot day" ("The Adventure of the Six Napoleons").

🔍Holmes not taking credit for solving Lestrade's cases (even truer in the books) is mentioned.

🔍Anderson seems to have turned from skeptic to believer. By contrast on *Elementary*, a cop under

Gregson instead becomes disillusioned with Holmes and never wants to see him again.

🐾In Germany, Holmes gets Trepoff convicted. "From time to time I heard some vague account of his doings: of his summons to Odessa in the case of the Trepoff murder," the story "A Scandal in Bohemia" mentions.

🐾The box Lestrade brings Watson has a yellow mask from the short story "The Yellow Face" as well as the pink cellphone from "A Study in Pink." There's an unknown piece of paper and a toy train engine. This last is unclear – there's a set of blocks in "The Man with the Twisted Lip" and a rattle and picture book in "The Greek Interpreter," plus trains feature in many cases. It even appears to date back to Victorian times.

🐾In his recorded birthday message for Watson, Holmes notes, "I wrote an essay on suppressed hatred in close proximity based entirely on his friends. On reflection, it probably wasn't a very good choice of gift." The monographs written on strange subjects (perfumes, cigar ash, malingering, footprints…) are a running joke through the books.

🐾The newspaper headline reads "The Game is Back On!" a nod to Sherlock's "The game is on!"

🐾Sherlock appears to answer John directly in the video – this also occurred in another Moffat episode, *Doctor Who*'s "Blink."

🐾Sherlock's video line, "I'm going to be with you again very soon" obviously has additional meaning as Holmes's return grows near.

SHERLOCK

THE EMPTY HEARSE

The Title

Originally, this is "The Empty House," site of a locked room murder. There's an additional empty house where Holmes lays a trap for Moriarty's final lieutenant, Colonel Moran. "The Empty Hearse" references Anderson's fan group, called this because they believe Sherlock never died and thus never traveled in a Hearse. They are correct of course.

The Story

Holmes has been dead for two years in the episode, three in the book. With a terrorist plot on the show, or a slipup by Colonel Moran in the books, he decides it's time to return to England. He startles Watson, and in the books, is instantly forgiven and they stake out Baker Street, where Holmes has placed a bust of his head. Moran shoots it; Holmes and Watson apprehend him with the remarkably long-range gun used in the locked room murder. Case closed. Watson's wife has died in the interim, and Holmes and Watson move back into Baker Street in the next story.

Gatiss wanted to have Watson react very differently from the original character at the discovery of Holmes's return in series three; "I always found it a little unlikely that Dr. Watson's only reaction was to faint for instance – as opposed to possibly a stream of terrible swear words," he said. ("Sherlock Series

Three"). Thus "The Empty Hearse" involves a long journey from fury to forgiveness for Watson. There's also a plot to blow up Parliament for Guy Fawkes Day and a mysterious criminal who tries to burn Watson alive, apparently to observe the situation.

Blog

Watson references the fandom, noting, "As the trending hashtag says: #sherlocklives" The blog also features a "news clip" revealing Sherlock's return. Watson notes, "Everything I've said on this blog has been the truth and now everyone knows it. I just want to take a minute to thank those who commented on here saying that they still believed in him. It really helped."

He lets loose with his emotions, adding,

> I was out having dinner with my girlfriend when he sauntered back into my world. He was dressed as a waiter. BECAUSE HE THOUGHT IT WOULD BE FUNNY. He genuinely thought it would be funny to surprise me. I think he was more surprised when I nutted him. But let's not dwell on that because again, as the saying goes, life goes on. (Watson's Blog, "The Empty Hearse")

As such, Watson offers deeper insights into his own character. Others post short comments: Mrs. Hudson gushes with satisfaction at seeing "her boys" together, and Molly confesses that she's no John Watson.

Symbolism: Trains

Trains often represent a journey in fiction. Towards the episode's beginning John rides the tube to Baker Street juxtaposed with Sherlock heading to Mycroft's office in the Diogenes Club. John is going to tell Mrs. Hudson he's getting married while Sherlock has just returned to London and plans to take up his old life again.

While Molly and Sherlock are investigating together, dust falls from the ceiling and Molly asks "trains?" At the same time as Sherlock is trying a new partner, he keeps hearing Watson's voice in his head, emphasizing how much trouble he's having with changing. Finally, Sherlock and Watson face a bomb in a train at the episode's climax. Trapped together, Sherlock acknowledged how he hurt Watson and honestly begs his forgiveness. Several times, John suspects a trick, but Sherlock convinces him they are going to die. John forgives him, and Sherlock reveals he actually was up to his "old tricks" – with the balance between them restored, everything has actually gone back to normal. They reunite with their friends at Baker Street, emphasizing that all their journeys have taken them straight back to the beginning. At the same time, the Moriarty era has ended at last, and Sherlock has become kinder (as shown by his not commenting on Molly's boyfriend). With Watson's fiancée present as well, the story is ready to move to new adventures and a new dynamic.

Canon References

🔺Having explained his Sherlock survival theory to Lestrade, Anderson talks about paving slabs outside Barts. This is an allusion to the solution to a Jonathan Creek mystery, "The Problem at Gallows Gate."

🔺In Serbia, Mycroft mentions Baron Maupertius from "The Reigate Puzzle." Mycroft adds that Sherlock's been "a busy little bee," referencing his future hobby.

🔺The Guy Fawkes plot is seen in several of Sherlock Holmes's radio dramas: In "The Guy Fawkes Society," Holmes goes undercover in a dangerous club to stop a plot again Parliament. In "The Gunpowder Plot" Guy Falconby plans to murder his cousin James Stuart by blowing him up on Guy Fawkes Day.

🔺In *The Case of the Silk Stocking* (2004), Watson and Holmes work alongside Watson's fiancée, an American psychoanalyst who's aggressive and lectures Holmes on her chosen subject. She's knowledgeable about her topic, but quite abrasive. Mary, by contrast, doesn't get involved in their cases, just offers helpful hints. She appears to want to preserve the two men's friendship. In the Robert Downey Jr. film, Mary looks like she'll come between the two men, but by the end of the case, she tells Holmes that they love Watson equally and need to save him. She's seen actively participating is the case of the sequel.

🐾Watson's mustache is iconic from the series and most adaptations, but here, everyone hates it.

🐾A newspaper article foreshadows the third episode, reading, "Magnussen summoned before parliamentary..."

🐾Sherlock admits: "Bit mean, springing it on you like that, I know. Could have given you a heart attack, probably still will. But in my defense, it was very funny." In the book, Watson faints and Holmes apologizes for being so dramatic.

🐾"You know my methods, Watson, I am well known to be indestructible" is a quote from the 1965 movie *A Study in Terror.*

🐾One of Holmes's planned escapes involves "a system of Japanese wrestling." In the books, that's the one he uses – the fictional martial art of baritsu.

🐾In "The Empty House," only Mycroft knew of Holmes' plot, because Holmes needed his money. Here it is Mycroft, their parents, Molly and 25 members of his homeless network. No wonder John decks him.

🐾Sherlock tells Watson: "I've nearly been in contact so many times, but I worried that, you know, you might say something indiscreet." In the short story, he says, "Several times during the last three years I have taken up my pen to write to you, but always I feared lest your affectionate regard for me should tempt you to some indiscretion which would betray my secret."

🐾Mrs. Hudson seems quite emotional at getting both men back in her life...in the Jeremy Brett adaptation of "The Empty House," she bursts into tears, and Holmes unbends enough to give her a hug.

Mary reads aloud from an old blog entry: "His movements were so silent. So furtive, he reminded me of a trained bloodhound picking out a scent...I couldn't help thinking what an amazing criminal he'd make if he turned his talents against the law." This is a scene from "The Sign of Four." Holmes mentions in several cases that he would have been a highly effective criminal.

Sherlock says in voiceover: "London. It's like a great cesspool into which all kinds of criminals, agents and drifters are irresistibly drained." Watson describes London thus in "A Study in Scarlet."

Sherlock notes: "I'll find the answer. It'll be in an odd phrase in an online blog, or an unexpected trip to the countryside, or a misplaced Lonely Hearts ad." In the books, Holmes uses the Agony Column (basically the personals) to track London's criminal pulse.

Sherlock tells Mycroft, "I'm just passing the time. Let's do deductions" and picks up an abandoned bobble hat. Holmes does this with a client's abandoned stick in "Hound of the Baskervilles" and an abandoned hat in "The Adventure of the Blue Carbuncle" just as an intellectual exercise. He plays against Mycroft in "The Greek Interpreter":

> "To anyone who wishes to study mankind this is the spot," said Mycroft. "Look at the magnificent types! Look at these two men who are coming towards us, for example."
> "The billiard-marker and the other?"
> "Precisely. What do you make of the other?"
> The two men had stopped opposite the window. Some chalk marks over the waistcoat pocket were the only signs of billiards which I could see in one of them. The other was a very small, dark fellow, with his hat pushed back and several packages under his arm.
> "An old soldier, I perceive," said Sherlock.
> "And very recently discharged," remarked the brother.
> "Served in India, I see."
> "And a non-commissioned officer."

"Royal Artillery, I fancy," said Sherlock.
"And a widower."
"But with a child."
"Children, my dear boy, children." ("The Greek
Interpreter")

🔺Sherlock reveals (possibly) how he faked his death.
Sherlock was actually playing with a bouncy ball in a
scene in "The Reichenbach Fall."
🔺The monographs written on strange subjects are a
running joke through the books. Also, Mrs. Hudson
offers the same line in *The Private Life of Sherlock Holmes*.

> SHERLOCK: I've written a blog on the varying
> tensile strengths of different natural fibres.
> MRS HUDSON: I'm sure there's a crying need for
> that.

🔺The quote "Elementary, my dear Watson" was made
popular by the film *The Adventures of Sherlock
Holmes* (1939). It was never featured in a
canonical Arthur Conan Doyle story. Perhaps this is
why the phrase hasn't be featured in *Sherlock*.

> SHERLOCK (sarcastically): Brilliant!
> MYCROFT: Elementary.

This exchange is adapted from "The Crooked Man":

> "Excellent!" I cried [Watson].
> "Elementary," said he [Holmes].

🔺MYCROFT: I'm not lonely, Sherlock. SHERLOCK:
How would you know? This nods back to a
conversation they have in "A Scandal in Belgravia."
🔺The monkey glands case is a nod to "The Adventure of
the Creeping Man."
🔺Spouses keeping secrets from each other appear in "The
Adventure of the Dancing Men" "The Yellow Face"
and "The Valley of Fear." Each time, an affair is

suspected, but the answer is something else. This episode reverses the trope:

> SHERLOCK: Why didn't you assume it was your wife?
> MR. HARCOURT: Because I've always had total faith in her.
> SHERLOCK: No – it's because you emptied it. (He points at the three areas on the man at which he had just looked and speaks quick-fire.) Weight loss, hair dye, Botox, affair. (Whipping out a business card, he holds it out to Mrs Harcourt.) Lawyer. Next!

🦇This case, in all its details but the online part, is a retelling of "A Case of Identity."

> SHERLOCK (softly): And you really thought he was the one, didn't you? The love of your life?
> (As the woman takes off her glasses and cries harder, Sherlock turns and looks at Molly for a moment, then stands and walks across to her. Keeping his back to the clients, he speaks quietly.)
> SHERLOCK: Stepfather posing as online boyfriend.
> MOLLY (shocked): What?!
> SHERLOCK: Breaks it off, breaks her heart. She swears off relationships, stays at home – he still has her wage coming in.
> (He turns to the man and addresses him sternly.)
> SHERLOCK: Mr. Windibank, you have been a complete and utter...

🦇"Doctor Verner is your usual GP, yes?" John asks. Following "The Empty House," a young doctor named Verner buys Watson's practice and Watson moves back in with Holmes: "A young doctor, named Verner, had...given with astonishingly little demur the highest price that I ventured to ask – an incident which only explained itself some years later when I found that Verner was a distant relation of Holmes's, and that it was my friend who had really found the money" ("The Adventure of the Norwood Builder").

🐾Mr. Szikora with a German accent, long white hair and a white beard, is wearing a black knitted hat and very dark glasses. He comes for a medical appointment and tries to sell John DVDs. John thinks it's Sherlock in disguise. In "The Empty House," this is the costume worn by Holmes when he surprises Watson with his reappearance. Holmes is also disguised as a German bookseller in *Sherlock Holmes and the Secret Weapon* (1943). After this, Watson tries to pull off a man's beard in *The Spider Woman* (1944), assuming it's Holmes again.

🐾Mr. Szikora offers John porn titled "British Birds" and "The Holy War." Holmes as the bookseller tells Watson, "Maybe you collect yourself, sir; here's *British Birds,* and *Catullus,* and *The Holy War* – a bargain every one of them. With five volumes you could just fill that gap on that second shelf. It looks untidy, does it not, sir?" thus getting him to turn his head.

🐾Sherlock is called in by Lestrade to deal with a fake Jack the Ripper skeleton. Holmes doesn't battle the Ripper in canon, but he's involved with the Ripper in many stories and films by later authors including *The Woman in Green* (1945), *A Study in Terror* (1965), *Murder by Decree* (1979) and *Dust and Shadow: An Account of the Ripper Killings* by Lyndsay Faye.

> SHERLOCK: I know a fantastic fish shop just off the Marylebone Road. The owner always gives me extra portions.
> MOLLY (following him): Did you get him off a murder charge?
> SHERLOCK: No – I helped him put up some shelves.

Mrs. Hudson and Angelo, by contrast, do owe Sherlock for his detective work.

🐾 Mary comes to Sherlock and tells him: "Someone sent me this. At first I thought it was just a Bible thing, you know, spam, but it's not. It's a skip-code." A third-word skip code features in "The 'Gloria Scott'."

🔺The code contains the phrase "John or James Watson." This nods to the fact that in the canon, Mary Morstan once called her husband John Watson "James."

🔺A bomb and an international plot appear in various films. In *Sherlock Holmes and the Leading Lady* (1991) in 1910, Mycroft asks Holmes and Watson to travel to Vienna and track down the stolen plans & prototype for an electro-magnetic bomb detonator.

🔺The train station stop is given as "Sumatra Road." Sherlock calls Moran the "Big Rat," and "Rat Number One" nodding to the untold story (and fan favorite) of the "Giant Rat of Sumatra."

> SHERLOCK: Lord Moran, peer of the realm,
> Minister for Overseas Development. Pillar of the
> establishment.
> JOHN: Yes!
> SHERLOCK: He's been working for North Korea
> since 1996.

In the book, the villain Colonel Sebastian Moran is Moriarty's number one lieutenant.

🔺The plot alludes to "The Lost Special," a Doyle story that appears to feature an unnamed Holmes as detective investigating a lost train car.

> SHERLOCK: They'll get in the way. They always do.
> This is cleaner, more efficient.
> (Stopping at a locked maintenance entrance, he
> reaches into his coat, takes out a crowbar and starts
> to force the gate open.)
> JOHN: And illegal.
> SHERLOCK: A bit.

In the books, Holmes is always picking locks and breaking into places. Occasionally, the police point out that they can't use these methods.

🔺The Houses of Parliament are to be blown up – in Robert Downey Jr.'s *Sherlock Holmes,* the men inside those Houses are to be poisoned.

John forgives Sherlock and tells him, "You were the best and the wisest man that I have ever known," in a direct quote from Watson's last homage to him in "The Final Problem."

Sherlock notes, "The criminal network Moriarty headed was vast. Its roots were everywhere like a cancer, so we came up with a plan." He says in the books: "The central power which uses the agent is never caught – never so much as suspected. This was the organization which I deduced, Watson, and which I devoted my whole energy to exposing and breaking up" ("The Final Problem"). In both scenes he mentions a spider in the web.

Actor Allusions

Amanda Abbington (Mary Morstan) is Martin Freeman's real-life partner.

Benedict Cumberbatch's parents (both actors themselves) appear as Sherlock's parents.

"Sauron1976" comments on John's blog around this time (Watson's Blog, "A Few Pictures"). Benedict Cumberbatch plays the Necromancer (the future Sauron) in *The Hobbit* and was born in 1976.

Sherlock fakes his death with the plan "Lazarus," with the aid of Mycroft, played by Mark Gatiss. Gatiss also starred in an episode of *Doctor Who* called "The Lazarus Experiment," in which he played Professor Richard Lazarus.

Innuendo

JOHN (smiling): Yeah. We're getting married...well, I'm gonna ask, anyway.
MRS HUDSON (looking more doubtful): So soon after Sherlock?
JOHN: Well, yes.

MRS HUDSON: What's his name?
JOHN (exasperated sigh): It's a woman.
MRS HUDSON: A woman?!
JOHN: Yes, of course it's a woman.
MRS HUDSON: You really have moved on, haven't you?
JOHN: Mrs. Hudson! How many times...? Sherlock was not my boyfriend.
MRS HUDSON (smiling affectionately): Live and let live – that's my motto.
JOHN (slowly getting louder): Listen to me: I am not gay!

British Culture

This episode features Guy Fawkes Day, with both an innocent celebration turned deadly and a repeat of the Gunpowder plot. Guy Fawkes conspired to assassinate King James I of England and the members of Parliament by blowing up the Parliament buildings during the ceremony of the State Opening of Parliament. He failed and was arrested on 5 November 1605. Effigies of him are burned in bonfires on Guy Fawkes Day through today. The popular associated rhyme (quoted by Watson) goes:

> Remember, remember, the 5th of November
> The Gunpowder Treason and plot;
> I see of no reason why Gunpowder Treason
> Should ever be forgot.
>
> Guy Fawkes, Guy Fawkes,
> 'Twas his intent.
> To blow up the King and the Parliament.
> Three score barrels of powder below.
> Poor old England to overthrow.

Pop Culture

Mycroft and Holmes play *Operation*, (though at first it appears to be the more adult chess) then their parents visit and Mycroft promises to take them to a matinee of *Les Mis*.

A male voice on the TV asks: "What freedoms exactly are we protecting if we start spying on our own people?

This is an Orwellian measure on a scale unprecedented..." ("The Empty Hearse"). This reference to *1984* and dystopia emphasizes the tyranny.

🔺Guy Fawkes Day, a repeat of blowing up Parliament, and the November rhyme famously feature in the popular *V for Vendetta*. The Orwellian comment helps tie these dystopias together.

🔺Mycroft describes *Les Miserables* saying, "But you don't understand the pain of it – the horror!" This appears to be a *Heart of Darkness* or *Apocalypse Now* reference.

THE SIGN OF THREE

The Title

This riffs on the original story of a pact between four men who signed their documents with "The Sign of Four." At episode's end, Sherlock plays on this with his big reveal of the "sign of three."

The Story

> Murder. Sorry, did I say murder? I meant to say marriage. But, you know, quite similar procedures when you think about it. The participants tend to know each other and it's assuming they want one of them dead. In fairness, murder is a lot quicker, though. ("The Sign of Three")

The original story features Jonathan Small taking revenge on his prison guard Major Sholto for stealing a vast treasure while he was in prison – Small and his three confederates had made him a treasure map and signed it with the "sign of four," making a deal that Sholto would get the treasure and return to save them but he never did. Sholto's partner, Captain Morstan, left behind a daughter named Mary, who asks Holmes and Watson to accompany her to see Sholto's heirs once the treasure is discovered. However, one Sholto brother has been murdered in a perfect locked room mystery. During the investigation, complete with capers and death-defying stunts, Watson falls for Mary and proposes. They wed at the story's end. The new version, of course, is the story of a wedding, and within it, several old cases that end up being related. Sherlock jumps from case to case as he realizes that "The Mayfly Man" and "The Bloody Guardsman" are linked – to John's old commander Major Sholto who's come out of his reclusive lifestyle for John's wedding and is set to be the Mayfly Man's next victim.

Sherlock notes in the episode: "But a word to the wise. Should any of you require the services of either of us, I will solve your murder. But it takes John Watson to save your life" ("The Sign of Three"). In fact, he and Watson together save a life as, possibly for the first time, Sherlock persuades a man not to kill himself before Watson offers medical treatment.

Only Jonathan Small, taking odd jobs while planning revenge against Sholto, is from the original mystery. He is arrested and everyone returns to the celebration, except Sherlock. Watson notes in the books that this is always the way of it. "The division seems rather unfair," I remarked. "You have done all the work in this business. I get a wife out of it, Jones gets the credit, pray what remains for you?" ("The Sign of Four"). Holmes retreats into his drugs and modern Sherlock slinks from the party, both alone.

Blog

Wow!!!!!!!!! What a day!!!!!! That was the best wedding ever!!!!!! Sherlock was amazing! Love is amazing! Fluffy clouds and little birds are amazing!!! It was all just like so amazing! I'm going to write up all about it here! Because you all love reading my blog because I'm such a good writer!!! (Watson's Blog, "The Sign of Three").

Clearly Watson is over the moon about his wedding. Of course, this is instantly subverted in the next paragraph:

Sorry. I can't do it any more. I was going to attempt to mimic John's style of writing for an entire blog post but life's too short. And I say that as someone who died over two years ago. Good evening everyone, this is Sherlock Holmes. (Watson's Blog, "The Sign of Three").

Symbolism: Sherlock's Palace

GATISS: [The Mind Palace] came about because I remember having in the midst – probably in Cornwall – in the midst of an absolute crisis of intractability, I said, "But he's got to find out what it is, but he can't just bloody look it up. What is it?" and you said, "Why don't we do a Mind Palace?" 'cause we'd both read Derren Brown's book.
RUSSELL TOVEY: What, the Mind Palace isn't a Conan Doyle thing?
MOFFAT: No, no. It's a really interesting idea. It's how you store information in your brain.
GATISS: Hannibal Lecter does it, and it's a real idea. ("The Hounds of Baskerville" DVD Commentary)

However, the creators couldn't show more than superimposed text in "The Hounds of Baskerville" – doing otherwise would be too expensive.

The Mind Palace appears in "The Sign of Three" as a courtroom with Mycroft as the judge to Sherlock's lawyer. The women Sherlock invites in play in a giant game of Guess Who? And stand like statues when he's not using them – a perfect audience, barely alive to him. Mycroft is unimaginably tall and large, barking demands which only serve to confuse Sherlock and disorient him, as shown by his behavior during his wedding speech – the most disconcerted he's ever appeared. Sherlock also mentions he's plotted Mycroft's death – their relationship is quite problematic. He finally dismisses Mycroft as the voice of his mind, insisting on Watson instead, with the words, "You keep me right."

This seems to be a single room in his mind palace, yet it's quite telling – He's playing childish games and using people while Mycroft looms as the parent to Sherlock's child. "Let's play murder," he says in the real world of the wedding. Sherlock rebelliously tells adult Mycroft, "I'm not a child anymore": in fact a truly childish thing to say. Many references to Sherlock's childishness appear in this episode:

SHERLOCK (sitting down in his chair): You bring me tea in the morning?
MRS HUDSON (pouring the tea): Well, where d'you think it came from?!
SHERLOCK: I don't know. I just thought it sort of happened.
MRS HUDSON: Your mother has a lot to answer for.
(She takes the cup and saucer over to him.)
SHERLOCK: Mm, I know. I have a list. Mycroft has a file.
...
MRS HUDSON (walking towards the door): I really am going to have a word with your mother.
SHERLOCK: You can if you like. She understands very little.

This may simply mean that Sherlock operates on a mental level far above her or it may relate to his relationship with her as a misunderstood child.

In this episode, John and Mary act somewhat like Sherlock's parents – embarrassed by his impolite behavior yet also fighting for his needs when there's a real crisis. In other episodes, John has also been overprotective of Sherlock, shooting the assailant in the first episode and hurling himself at Moriarty so Sherlock can escape in "The Great Game." He tucks Sherlock into bed and is very protective of his feelings on discovering that Irene faked her death. Sherlock in turn acts completely panicked when John is threatened, showing that he might lose his only stability.

Before the wedding, Mary comforts Sherlock, pointing out that he shouldn't be jealous of John's having a friend before in Major Sholto. All three work as a team to save the Major, entering a new level of partnership – a real "Sign of Three."

Sherlock's adult confusion at Irene Adler (possibly a frequent guest in his mind palace) and Janine the maid of honor appear here – in the final minutes he appears ready to ask the Janine for a dance before seeing she has someone already.

Another example of Sherlock's childlike confusion appears during his first real conversation seen with a child:

SHERLOCK: Basically it's a cute smile to the bride's side, cute smile to the groom's side and then the rings.

ARCHIE: No.
SHERLOCK: And you have to wear the outfit.
ARCHIE: No.
SHERLOCK: You really do have to wear the outfit.
ARCHIE: What for?
SHERLOCK: Grown-ups like that sort of thing.
ARCHIE: Why?
(Sherlock pauses for a moment.)
SHERLOCK:...I don't know. I'll ask one.
ARCHIE (thoughtfully): You're a detective.
SHERLOCK: Yep.
ARCHIE: Have you solved any murders?
SHERLOCK: Sure. Loads.
ARCHIE: Can I see?
SHERLOCK (after only a momentary hesitation): Yeah, all right.

Sherlock implies that he understands being a boy but must consult a "real" adult on adult matters. He and Archie bond over gruesome case photos as Sherlock doesn't sugar-coat or sensor the images as other adults would.

By the episode's end he emphasizes his relationship with John and Mary, along with a hint of wistful jealousy:

SHERLOCK: Don't panic. None of you panic. Absolutely no reason to panic.
JOHN: Oh, and you'd know, of course?
SHERLOCK: Yes I would. You're already the best parents in the world, look at all the practice you've had.
JOHN: What practice?
SHERLOCK: Well, you're hardly going to need me around now that you've got a real baby on the way. ("The Sign of Three")

Canon References

🔺Donovan warns Lestrade: "Jones'll get all the credit if you leave now! You know he will!" Lestrade and Gregson spend the first episode battling to outdo each other on a case, and Jones is similar in "The Sign of Four."

🔺Holmes is shown getting on quite well with a little boy. On the show, he and the Baker Street Irregulars (a gang of street urchins) understand one another perfectly. This also works well as a nod to the film, *Sherlock Holmes and the Baker Street Irregulars*, which details more about the relationship.

🏔️John references Harry and her drinking problem, mentioned in the first episode. He also mentions he's seeing the psychiatrist less.

🏔️Wedding telegrams echo the original Holmes's fondness for telegrams.

🏔️One telegram Sherlock reads says, "...Oodles of love and heaps of good wishes from C.A.M. Wish your family could have seen this." Mary flinches. It appears she's had dealings with Charles Augustus Magnussen (Milverton in the short story). This also hints at her family situation – Mary notes in flashback that she's an orphan.

🏔️Sherlock reads a telegram from Mike Stamford, Watson's former colleague at Barts, who introduced them.

🏔️When Sherlock is asked to be a best man, he's confused and notes that a philanthropist (and occasional murderer) is the "best man" he knows:

> JOHN: The best man.
> SHERLOCK: The best man?
> JOHN: What do you think?
> SHERLOCK: Billy Kincaid.
> JOHN: Sorry, what?
> SHERLOCK: Billy Kincaid, the Camden Garroter. Best man I ever knew. Vast contributions to charity, never disclosed. Personally managed to save three hospitals from closure, and ran the best and safest children's homes in North England. Yes, every now and again there'd be some garrotings, but, stacking up the lives saved against the garrotings, on balance I'd say...

This is a flip on the original line – "I assure you that the most winning woman I ever knew was hanged for poisoning three little children for their insurance-money, and the most repellant man of my acquaintance is a philanthropist who has spent nearly a quarter of a million upon the London poor." ("The Sign of Four")

⚰Everyone warns Holmes that the relationship will change. This is the case in the books, as Watson loses track of many of Holmes's cases and only drops in on his occasionally during his marriage. At the end of "The Sign of the Four," Watson says, "I fear that it may be the last investigation in which I shall have the chance of studying your methods. Miss Morstan has done me the honor to accept me as a husband in prospective."

⚰Holmes replies with the line he repeats several times in the episode: "I really cannot congratulate you." Of course, in the book he says it in private, and on the show, he amends his answer, and finally adds that he actually does congratulate them.

⚰Holmes's other line from original story is repeated: "Love is an emotional thing, and whatever is emotional is opposed to that true cold reason which I place above all things" ("The Sign of the Four"). The wedding guests are not amused.

⚰In the book Holmes is not seen attending the wedding – it's uncertain that he even does so. It's certainly believable that he would compose a violin piece, practice dancing until it's exact, be immune to the bridesmaid's charms (yet size up the men around them), catch a criminal during the reception, and then finally walk off alone into the darkness.

⚰Speaking to young Archie, Sherlock says, "Get this right and there's a headless nun in it for you." This nods to the series' unaired pilot.

⚰The cases mentioned in this one do not appear to be in the book: "The Hollow Client," "The Matchbox Decathlete," "The Mayfly Man," "The Poison Giant," "The Bloody Guardsman," and "The Elephant in the Room." The last of these appears to be just a play on words with the expression "elephant in the room," except that "The Mystery of the Vanishing White Elephant" was a case in Basil Rathbone's *New Adventures of Sherlock Holmes* radio show of the 1940s. "The Mayfly Man" and "The Bloody Guardsman" are solved in the course of this episode.

⚜ "The Mayfly Man" has elements of "A Case of Identity," where a woman dates a mystery man who dumps her suddenly...it's her own stepfather, scaring off suitors (This plot also appears in "The Empty Hearse"). Likewise in "The Adventure of Charles Augustus Milverton," Holmes starts "walking out" with a housemaid and even proposes marriage just to get information on the man she works for (foreshadowing the following episode). This is the actual solution.

⚜ Sherlock tells of "The Matchbox Decathlete" – a French decathlete found surrounded by 1,812 matchboxes, all empty except one. "The Inexplicable Matchbox" appears on John's blog, There, he mentions Sherlock dressing as a clown and Mrs. Hudson being pushed from a helicopter. He's unable to add details due to "Every Official Secrets Act." This is adapted from the case "of Isadora Persano, the well-known journalist and duelist, who was found stark staring mad with a match box in front of him which contained a remarkable worm said to be unknown to science" ("The Problem of Thor Bridge").

⚜ Lestrade hypothesizes a very small person with a blow-pipe snuck through the vents and murdered the soldier for "The Bloody Guardsman," as Sherlock calls it. "The Poison Giant" has a similar plot. In "The Sign of Four," Jonathan Small's Pacific Islander accomplice fits this description, and this is actually how the murder was committed.

⚜ The locked room mystery death of "The Bloody Guardsman" also resembles "The Crooked Man" with a soldier out for revenge on another.

⚜ "The Hollow Client" is one of the cases on John's blog, explained fully there.

⚜ There's also the young woman who keeps hesitating on the pavement. Sherlock comments, "Oscillation on the pavement always means there's a love affair." "A Case of Identity" has the same line: "I have seen those symptoms before," said Holmes, throwing his cigarette into the fire. "Oscillation upon the pavement always means an *affaire de coeur*. She would like advice, but is not sure that the matter is not too delicate for communication."

🔍The fan joke about Watson's middle name appears again.

> GATISS: "Hamish" is from the Rathbone films, isn't it?
> MOFFAT: No. Doyle when he wrote these stories was appalling on continuity. Continuity was so bad, he once forgot Doctor Watson's name and had his wife call him James. He's called James for a whole story!
> CUMBERBATCH: Maybe she just forgot the name!
> MOFFAT: Someone came up with this brilliant theory that the middle name was Hamish – 'cause it's John H. Watson in the stories – and Hamish is the Scottish version of James, so she called him by his middle name.
> …
> GATISS: What's great is, the lack of Doyle's continuity is a great field for in-jokes.
> (Commentary, "A Scandal in Belgravia")

🔍For the second episode running, Sherlock gets Lestrade's first name wrong: Gavin this time, Graham in "The Empty Hearse." Doyle only ever referred to 'G. Lestrade,' though he's named Greg for Inspector Gregson.

🔍"Vatican cameos" (Watson and Holmes' code phrase for danger) appears again along with a quick glimpse of Irene Adler from the same episode.

🔍Sherlock calls himself a high-functioning sociopath again, nodding to episode one.

🔍Holmes asks Molly about her boyfriend while studying how to get only mildly drunk.

🔍Molly calls Sherlock a graduate chemist. Watson remarks on his friend's knowledge of chemistry and wonders if he's a student in the first story.

🔍Sherlock mentions his "international reputation."

🔍In his speech, Sherlock describes a case he failed to solve. These happen occasionally, but rarely. "I have been beaten four times – three times by men, and once by a woman," Sherlock admits ("The Five Orange Pips"). In "The Yellow Face" he simply gets the case completely wrong.

🔍Watson's military career is mentioned, though it fails to get him any concessions.

🔍Both Captain Sholtos (original and from this episode) are guilty of great betrayals.

🔍Sherlock lets the phrase "previous commander" slip out, suggesting he's Watson's current commander. He does on occasion act like it, even in the books:

> "Good morning, Holmes," said the baronet. "You look like a general who is planning a battle with his chief of the staff."
> "That is the exact situation. Watson was asking for orders."
> "And so do I." ("The Hound of the Baskervilles")

In "The Illustrious Client," Watson notes, "He gave no explanations and I asked for none. By long experience I had learned the wisdom of obedience."

🔍A client writes "my husband is three people," and Holmes intuits triplets. Identical twin criminals appear in the film *The Case of the Silk Stocking* (2004).

🔍Sherlock claims he learned napkin folding at an operahouse. An operahouse case appears in *Sherlock Holmes and the Leading Lady* (1991).

🔍When Sherlock is drunk, the text surrounding his observations is ridiculously useless, emphasizing his current state.

🔍Sherlock mentions he's drugged Watson successfully before – this is seen in "The Hounds of Baskerville."

Robert Downey Jr.'s *Sherlock Holmes* also has Watson and Holmes ending an era as Watson moves out and plans to marry. Mary in the movie says, "I know you care for him as much as I do...Solve this. Whatever it takes." In this episode Mary shares both these last two sentiments.

Pop Culture

Holmes has a Sudoku puzzle cube.

John must guess that he's supposed to be "Madonna," but Sherlock doesn't actually know who she is.

"There should always be a spectre at the feast," Sherlock says, meaning Mycroft. This references Banquo's disturbing appearance at the feast of *Macbeth*.

The glowing matchbox may be a *Pulp Fiction* reference.

Innuendo

John calls Sherlock and Mary "the two people that I love and care about most in the world." He adds that both Sherlock and Mary have completely changed his life.

Sherlock calls John "the bravest and kindest and wisest human being I have ever had the good fortune of knowing."

> John, I am a ridiculous man. Redeemed only by the warmth and constancy of your friendship....So know this: today you sit between the woman you have made your wife and the man you have saved. In short, the two people who love you most in all this world. And I know I speak for Mary as well when I say we will never let you down, and we have a lifetime ahead to prove that.

Many of Sherlock's comments, and his similarities with calculating, clever Mary, foreshadow this season's final episode.

"We can't all three of us dance. There are limits," is said at the wedding. In *Sherlock Holmes and the Leading Lady* (1991), Irene Adler suggests Holmes pretend to be her lover. He agrees and asks, "What about Watson?" She blinks and tells him, "Sherlock, there are limits, even in Vienna." The line may be a callback to this film.

Doctor Who

Sherlock's frenetic babble when he corrects himself after his Sign of Three slip-up or when the case intrudes on his speech resembles the Doctor's. "Love a wedding!" he bursts out unconvincingly, mimicking many of the Doctor's phrases ("Love an ood!").

In this episode and in Moffat's "The Doctor Dances" Sherlock and the Doctor both enjoy dancing and seem to resent being thought of asexual when interacting with Rose or Janine. Dancing and sex are a metaphor for each other in the *Doctor Who* episode.

When Sherlock gets drunk and scans the area, the usual deductions are replaced by words like "Chair? Sitty thing?" "Speaker high tech thing." The Tenth and Eleventh Doctors sometimes talk like this, as the Tenth says, "This is my timey-wimey detector. It goes ding when there's stuff" ("Blink").

British Culture

Wedding Telegrams are sent by those who can't make the ceremony and are often read aloud by the best man. Sherlock notes, "They're not actually telegrams. We just *call* them telegrams. I don't know why. Wedding tradition...because we don't have enough of that already, apparently."

Archie is the page boy. These are traditional at British weddings, roughly equivalent to the American job of ringbearer.

🔺 The classic line to finish the wedding toast is something like "Ladies and Gentlemen, please be upstanding and charge your glasses. I give you: The bride and groom." Sherlock of course attempts this but then has an epiphany.

🔺 Other traditions like the white gown (popularized by Queen Victoria herself) are shared between Britain and the U.S. Others are a bit different: British women often wear hats to weddings (seen in Mrs. Hudson and some of the episode's other guests). The British say, "Something old, something new, something borrowed, something blue, a silver sixpence in her shoe." Waltzing and formality (such as Sherlock's properly escorting the maid of honor) are more common in the U.K. The stag night is about the same as a bachelor party.

🔺 The Changing of the Guard features heavily in the episode. This ceremony is still held roughly every other day outside Buckingham Palace by The Queen's Guard. They are a tourist attraction in themselves, considered British icons. Many tourists try to tease them or make them laugh, as they're famously stoic, something Sherlock and John discuss.

🔺 "Am I the current king of England?" Holmes asks when playing the Post-it Note game. Obviously, there's no such person, and hasn't been in Holmes's lifetime.

SHERLOCK

HIS LAST VOW

The Title

The title plays with "His Last Bow," Holmes's final case in the short stories (though fans have been assured series four will happen). This also nods to his "last vow" in the previous episode – that he will protect John, Mary and their baby, no matter the cost.

Symbolism: Inner Life

Jungian psychology involves facing one's dream imagery – the "little voices" of praise and criticism one finds deep within. Sherlock of course, encounters all these within his mind palace. There he is a small child again, and Mycroft is larger than life, censuring him about all the ways he's wrong. Molly is Sherlock's desperate, emotional need to live. Anderson pokes holes and criticizes. Encouraged to find a happy memory, he is young and carefree with his dog. He faces his fear – himself dead in a morgue – and the pain and shock of being shot.

At last Sherlock sinks into the basement of his palace, the place that reflects the subconscious. There, his greatest enemy Moriarty is chained. He represents the shadow – the raging, suppressed dark side of the personality. While many heroes avoid this facet of their deepest selves and refuse to face it, the shadow offers surprising strengths. Moriarty taunts Sherlock with his forthcoming death, and then finally reminds him that if he dies, John will be in terrible danger. At these words, Sherlock is galvanized. He drags himself up through his mind, stair by painful stair, back into the world of life.

This confrontation generally occurs in fiction in context of the hero's journey – the hero dies or has a near-death experience and crosses over to a world of thought and imagination: Harry Potter at King's Cross, Gandalf and the Balrog. Each time, the hero refuses to give up his destiny and returns to the world stronger, with new purpose. Thus Sherlock returns, and finally confronts the vile blackmailer.

Sherlock has more Jungian shadows than ever in this episode – people who observe in the same manner he does. Magnussen is the obvious one, with his mental dossiers much as Sherlock has. But Wiggins, Sherlock's new assistant, is seen doing the same. Mary too has a similar skillset. Even Janine is using Sherlock the way he used her. With all these geniuses, each using Sherlock's powers to commit immoral acts, Sherlock must become a hero – a knight who slays dragons, the champion of England...for a great threat is coming with the eastern wind.

The Story

In the original story, "The Adventure of Charles Augustus Milverton," Holmes negotiates with a seedy blackmailer to save a titled lady, Lady Eva Brackwell, in danger of having her marriage ruined by some imprudent letters. As Holmes describes him:

> He is the king of all the blackmailers. Heaven help the man, and still more the woman, whose secret and reputation come into the power of Milverton. With a smiling face and a heart of marble he will squeeze and squeeze until he has drained them dry. The fellow is a genius in his way, and would have made his mark in some more savoury trade. His method is as follows: He allows it to be known that he is prepared to pay very high sums for letters which compromise people of wealth or position. He receives these wares not only from treacherous valets or maids, but frequently from genteel ruffians who have gained the confidence and affection of trusting women.

When Milverton won't lower his price, Holmes resolves to break into his home and steal the letters, and Watson is determined to go along. They succeed in cracking the safe, but are interrupted when a different highborn lady slips in and murders Milverton for his crimes against her. Holmes and Watson burn all the letters, make a daring escape, and express to Lestrade over breakfast the next morning that Milverton's murder won't be solved by them.

In both stories, Watson is truly appalled when he discovers Sherlock has only been pretending to date a young woman and has even proposed, just to gain access to her boss. "Did you just get engaged just to get into an office?" John demands on the show. Sherlock blithely replies that he plans to confess and be dumped, thus everything will work out. In the short story, the young woman is never seen, but on the show, Janine returns for a delightful revenge.

Using the young lady, Sherlock breaks into Magnussen's stronghold. As in the short story, he discovers he's planned his burglary the same night the blackmailer's victim has planned his murder. However, Mary doesn't shoot Magnussen, but Sherlock. From there, Sherlock must work out a way to free his friends from the blackmailer's slimy grip. He offers to betray his country to save them, selling state secrets as he does in "The Last Bow." Both stories, of course, allow him to use this excuse to get close to the villain and end the threat to England in spectacular fashion.

Canon References

    Sherlock says, "I've dealt with murderers, psychopaths. None of them can turn my stomach like Charles Augustus Magnussen." In the original, Holmes calls Milverton "The worst man in London," and adds that "he is as cunning as the Evil One."

    Milverton lives at Appledore Towers in the original, like the security vault's name. His files and papers, neat little bundles of letters tied with ribbons, have been updated to a more elaborate system of storage.

- The Jeremy Brett adaptation shows Milverton living in a "fortress" with an iron gate, much like Magnussen's stronghold. The round glasses appear here, as well as in the original tale, but in Brett's and the short story, he's a pleasanter person.

- In the Brett version, Watson suggests getting involved in a scandal to drawn the blackmailer out. In the opium den, Sherlock seems to have a similar plan.

- In the books, he signs his notes C.A.M., like the wedding telegram he sends in "The Sign of Three."

- Sherlock calls him the "Napoleon of blackmail," just as Moriarty is the "Napoleon of crime." This may also foreshadow the episode's end.

- Sherlock adds in the short story that "He will hold a card back for years in order to play it at the moment when the stake is best worth winning." Certainly, C.A.M. is seen toying with Mary as he sends her a wedding telegram.

- Magnussen sizes up people, not for their habits, but for their pressure points. Sherlock suggests at one point that the text the audience sees is *actual* text from the man's spectacles, not the man's thoughts as they are Sherlock's. Both men have mind palaces, and seem to have similar skillsets, just ones they use quite differently.

- The highborn lady in the original authorizes Holmes to act as her agent and buy back the imprudent letters she wrote to a man. This time, she wants the letters her husband wrote to a woman. These letters are described varyingly as "lively" and "sprightly" in the two versions.

- John's flashback war dreams parallel the very first moments of "A Study in Pink." He also has a flashback to Sherlock's lines from the first episode asking if he wants to see more action.

- In the books, Mr. and Mrs. Watson sit happily at home, when there's a ring at the door.

> "Our own door flew open, and a lady, clad in some dark-coloured stuff, with a black veil, entered the room.
>
> "You will excuse my calling so late," she began, and then, suddenly losing her self-control, she ran forward, threw her arms about my wife's neck, and sobbed upon her shoulder. "Oh, I'm in such trouble!" she cried; "I do so want a little help."
>
> "Why," said my wife, pulling up her veil, "it is Kate Whitney. How you startled me, Kate! I had not an idea who you were when you came in."
>
> "I didn't know what to do, so I came straight to you." That was always the way. Folk who were in grief came to my wife like birds to a light-house.

Her husband, Isa Whitney, is at an opium den. Watson goes to retrieve the man, and finds Sherlock prowling there, on a case ("The Man with the Twisted Lip"). This episode contains the same scene, followed by an extensive drug test for Sherlock. This time it's "early" not late, and John guesses it's her husband, but it's her son "Isaac."

🥾Mycroft complains that their parents want to watch (or possibly visit) *Oklahoma* and not join Sherlock for an intervention. "It won't be the first time your habit has interfered with their line dancing." The parents and the drugs have both been introduced in previous episodes.

🥾The Christmas celebration nods back to the one of "A Scandal in Belgravia." Both times, Mycroft shows a loathing for the holiday.

🥾"You were gone. I saw an opportunity," Sherlock says of moving John's chair. Both Sherlock and various criminals say this line or a similar one in the stories.

🥾Later, Sherlock moves the chair back, possibly hinting that John is welcome to leave his wife and move back in. In the time between Sherlock's collapse and the Christmas party (it's unclear how much time has elapsed), Watson may do just that.

🥾Sherlock met Janine at the wedding of the previous episode. She mentions she knows him better than anyone, and indeed, he was being very much his true self at the reception.

🔺Sherlock notes that John's gained seven pounds.

"It's actually four pounds"

"No, I think seven."

> "Wedlock suits you," he remarked. "I think, Watson, that you have put on seven and a half pounds since I saw you."
> "Seven!" I answered.
> "Indeed, I should have thought a little more. Just a trifle more, I fancy, Watson. ("A Scandal in Bohemia")

One of Watson's pressure points is listed as the alcoholic sister (mentioned in several episodes), the other as his wife.

🔺Sherlock's porn preference is stated as "normal" (that seems uncharacteristic). His finances are "unknown" – this is constant with the stories. Though he appears to be an impoverished near-student in need of a roommate for a small three-room apartment in "A Study in Scarlet," he uses bribery constantly as a tool and takes cabs throughout London. In fact, he shows very little instances of poverty outside of his introduction to Watson. After his fame increases, he mentions he's become enormously well off and need never work again.

🔺Sherlock's pressure points appear a near-endless list – Irene Adler, Jim Moriarty, Redbeard, Hounds of the Baskerville, Opium, John Watson. Oddly, Mycroft is not listed – perhaps this villain only harms the most vulnerable.

🔺Irene Adler does appear to be a pressure point for Sherlock, either because Magnussen knows she's alive or because he knows Sherlock unwittingly helped her. Moriarty is less clear, unless he is in fact alive as well. Redbeard appears to be a dog and appears to be deceased, based on Mycroft's previous remarks...could Redbeard be involved in some dark incident, like criminal charges or the mysterious story of the third Holmes sibling? Hounds of the Baskerville is also a puzzle – is this about Sherlock breaking in with government ID? Or keeping the project secret after the case? Or the far deeper secret that Sherlock fears losing his emotional distance more than anything? Sherlock has not been described as taking opium on the show, and in the books he assures Watson he's not adding the drug to his other vices. This may be the drug he once used to take, and this episode also has a nod to the opium den case, "The Man with the Twisted Lip." Watson as pressure point will become important by episode end.

⚜Sherlock is visibly shaken at the reference to Redbeard. This story will probably emerge in series four.

⚜Mycroft enlists Sherlock's fan club to search for drugs, then threatens them with the British Secret Service...his political power is emphasized here. He appears to be in M.I.6. He does not have this role in the books, but has one like it in *The Private Life of Sherlock Holmes*. Magnussen may reference the movie briefly when he refuses to offer Sherlock and John an expensive beverage. In the movie, Mycroft pours the two men a very expensive drink, as they so rarely visit. There's also a very rare wine served in "His Last Bow" – Holmes and Watson share it after tying up their host.

⚜Bill Wiggins goes from manager of a drug den to a homeless man who's actually working for Holmes and calls himself Sherlock's "protégé." In the books, Wiggins is the head of the Baker Street Irregulars – a gang of street children, and Billy is Holmes's pageboy. He may provide a new amusing character in the episodes to come.

⚜In the story, Holmes says, "Do you feel a creeping, shrinking sensation, Watson, when you stand before the serpents in the Zoo and see the slithery, gliding, venomous creatures, with their deadly eyes and wicked, flattened faces? Well, that's how Milverton impresses me. I've had to do with fifty murderers in my career, but the worst of them never gave me the repulsion which I have for this fellow." Sherlock uses many of these words when comparing the updated villain to a shark in a tank.

🔺Mrs. Hudson gets the door for their client, something she does constantly in the books and rarely so far on the show.

🔺In the short story, Sherlock shops for burglary tools; on the show, he shops for a diamond ring.

> JOHN: We should call the police!
> SHERLOCK: During our own burglary? You're really not a natural at this, are you?

In the short story, instead, Holmes says, "I can see that you have a strong natural turn for this sort of thing."

🔺Sherlock recognizes *clare de lune* perfume (and misses crucial foreshadowing when John mentions that Mary wears it). His perfume knowledge appears earlier and is referenced in the books: "There are seventy-five perfumes, which it is very necessary that a criminal expert should be able to distinguish from each other, and cases have more than once within my own experience depended upon their prompt recognition," he says in "The Hound of the Baskervilles."

🔺The white supremacist guard may be a nod to "The Five Orange Pips."

🔺The evil white lights seen in "The Hounds of Baskerville" appear in Sherlock's mind palace as he goes into shock. He also thinks briefly of Irene Adler and is taunted by Moriarty. There's a childhood scene with his dog, who appears to be a pleasant memory. Mycroft as his judge returns from the previous episode.

🔺Janine gets rid of the beehives in her new cottage, nodding to Sherlock's retirement hobby.

🔺Mary keeps her background on a drive labeled A.G.R.A. – in the book she meets John because she's seeking the great Agra treasure. The treasure is lost forever, and thus John feels able to court Mary, who's no longer an heiress. By burning the A.G.R.A. disk, without reading it, this John feels he can have her back.

🔺 Sherlock tells John *not* to bring a gun on a dangerous adventure, then to bring a gun to his parents' Christmas party. Bringing the gun is Watson's job in the books.

🔺 John notes, "Try finding Sherlock in London." In the books, he has boltholes and hiding places, with an amazing talent for disguises and friends in high and low places.

🔺 Their mother mentions if she finds the man who "put a bullet" in her boy, she'll turn "absolutely monstrous." She's written the book *The Dynamics of Combustion*, which suggests explosives. Mr. Holmes mentions her genius directly after this, but Sherlock and Mycroft clearly get more than brains from the woman, who has a well-developed dark side. In the book series, Sherlock will eventually become an author as well.

🔺 Sherlock relies on Mary being clever. He's done this with Irene and Moriarty on the show, and with several characters in the books.

🔺 There are flashbacks to Mary's cleverness in the previous two episodes, as well as Magnussen's bonfire trick.

🔺 "Sorry, I never could resist a touch of drama," Sherlock tells Mary after posting her face on the side of a building. "My old friend here will tell you that I have an impish habit of practical joking. Also that I can never resist a dramatic situation," he says in "The Adventure of the Mazarin Stone."

🔺 Sherlock stresses the abandoned buildings (seen in "The Empty House," and appears to use the same strategy he uses in the short story, distracting his assailant with a bust of himself. In fact, the audience have been fooled, and John is the one hidden there.

🔺 In the books, Holmes burgles Milverton's house and destroys his files. As he tells Watson, "Since it is morally justifiable I have only to consider the question of personal risk. Surely a gentleman should not lay much stress upon this when a lady is in most desperate need of his help?" This episode emphasizes Sherlock's chivalry, as a "slayer of dragons" who loathes the bully who preys on the weak. In the original, he was prepared to brave jail for a titled lady who's a near-stranger – How else then could he act this time with John, Mycroft, and a pregnant Mary is even worse danger?

🔺Sherlock's status as a high-functioning sociopath and the violence he'll do when someone threatens his friends appear (remember the thugs who roughed up Mrs. Hudson).

🔺In the previous episode, Sherlock made, as he calls it, "My first, and last, vow. Mary and John – whatever it takes, whatever happens, from now on, I swear I will always be there. Always." In the episode, Sherlock is surprisingly kind to Mary, offering his help repeatedly. He makes sure John learns the truth, but counsels him to hear her out fairly, and points out John is less innocent than he had thought. Sherlock also appears to invite John over without telling him Mary's coming to make them work out their problems. Sherlock appears to understand Mary – a brilliant, amoral person who nonetheless loves John and wants to protect him. As a final step in his vow, Sherlock actually chooses not to be there ever again…in return for saving Mary and John from the blackmailer.

🔺"Give my love to Mary," Sherlock says. "Tell her she's safe now." In his goodbye letter of "The Final Problem," Sherlock writes, "My best to Mrs. Watson."

🔺In both stories, C.A.M. is convinced he's foolproof and that no one will shoot him. He's proven wrong.

🔺JOHN: The Game is over. SHERLOCK: The game is never over, John. But there may be some new players now. This of course references their constant references to "the game is on." Mary has the potential to be a fascinating player, as does this newer, harder John Watson.

- Sherlock's joke that he's always wanted to tell John something echoes John's words by Sherlock's grave.
- The spying in Eastern Europe Sherlock is to go on is straight from His Last Bow. Holmes notes in the story, "The Foreign Minister alone I could have withstood, but when the Premier also deigned to visit my humble roof – !" In the episode, the heads of the government send him off as well.
- Mycroft actually references another brother, noting, "Look how the other one turned out." The book *Sherlock Holmes of Baker Street* by Baring-Gould creates a third brother, who became the family's country squire. He's named Sherrinford after one of Doyle's rejected names for his hero. The film *Sherlock Holmes's Smarter Brother* (1975) is a farce about Siegerson, who blunders about and only thinks he's a great detective. If there is a third brother, one presumes he will have a more serious story on *Sherlock*. It would be unsurprising to find he's a criminal mastermind or died tragically.
- Mycroft mentions a colleague who uses people as "blunt instruments" – this is M in *Casino Royale*.
- Sherlock mentions he's "William Sherlock Scott Holmes" if John needs a baby name. John says something similar in "A Scandal in Belgravia." This may nod to Benedict Timothy Carlton Cumberbatch.
- "William Sherlock Scott Holmes" is Sherlock's name in the Wold Newton family, an experiment that connects fictional characters' family trees. One of his descendants, for instance, is said to be Spock, on his human mother's side. It's also notable that the Holmes parents called their children "Mike" and "William" – only the boys create more complex identities.
- Sherlock says he has a girl's name. In fact, *The Adventures of Shirley Holmes* was a television show in Canada.
- The line of the scary east wind, repeated several times, is from "His Last Bow," a story that takes place on the eve of World War I: "There's an east wind coming all the same, such a wind as never blew on England yet. It will

be cold and bitter, Watson, and a good many of us may wither before its blast. But it's God's own wind none the less, and a cleaner, better, stronger land will lie in the sunshine when the storm has cleared." This metaphor of trouble from the east means the war, but the promise of a better time to follow is reassuring for fans of Sherlock's world.

🔺Sherlock's becoming a murderer was actually foreshadowed in the first episode.

🔺Targeting lasers brush over Sherlock, as they did at the end of the first series. This time, however, they belong to his brother.

🔺The question over last season's break was "How did Sherlock survive St. Bart's." This time it's "How did Moriarty survive St. Bart's."

🔺Of course, there's no evidence Moriarty is alive – this hoax could be put on by any number of villains (like the yet unseen Moran) or allies – Sherlock, Mycroft, Irene, Mary, or Sherlock's fan club could have perpetuated a hoax to keep Sherlock in the country. The timing seems significant.

Actor Allusions
Young Sherlock in "His Last Vow" is Moffat's younger son Louis.

British Culture
The Danish criminal seems to be attacking England itself – not just its ministers, but also its manners and rules of decent behavior. "You're so domesticated. All standing around and apologizing. Keeping your little heads down," he mocks. Holmes has an answer to this in "His Last Bow" when he tells a German agent, "The Englishman is a patient creature, but at present his temper is a little inflamed, and it would be as well not to try him too far." In this episode he has an answer as well, as he confronts the bully at last.

THE BLOG CASES

The Six Thatchers

The Blog features "The Six Thatchers" obviously a retelling of "The Six Napoleons." Sally Barnicot who brings them the case, is adapted from Dr. Barnicot, whose two busts of Napoleon are smashed. "Pietro Venucci, an art student, and Sally's best friend had been found stabbed in the pottery room. His boyfriend, Beppo Rovito, was discovered next to the body and told the police that he'd just discovered him." Both of these characters take similar roles of murderer and victim in this original story, though Beppo has no last name given.

> Sherlock requested, or rather ordered, me to go to the university, pretending to be a curator from the Hickman Gallery. I told the art lecturer, Horace Harker, that I was interested in displaying some students' work - especially pieces of sculpture.
> We followed him to a bridge and watched as he smashed the figure to the ground. Something was inside it which he picked up, ready to throw in the river. Before he could, we stopped him and found that he was holding a penknife with his initials on it.
> Knowing that it was all over, he confessed immediately. He and Pietro had had an argument and, in a struggle, Beppo had stabbed him. He'd seen the figures were about to go into the oven and had pushed the knife into the clay. He'd then smashed a window to make it look like there'd been a break-in.

The Hollow Client

Jack Griffin visits to consult, but only his suit remains there, suggesting he's turned invisible – the very problem he had previously emailed Sherlock about. After going through many complex theories: mirrors, invisible paint, fabric matching, drugs, holograms...Watson arrives at the real solution – that all this is a practical joke.

Strange occurrences are thought to be practical jokes in "The Red-Headed League," "The Adventure of Wisteria Lodge," "The Hound of the Baskervilles," "The Adventure of the Cardboard Box," and "The Adventure of the Dancing Men," but are actually far graver. Criminals in "The Norwood Builder" and "A Case of Identity" claim they were only pulling jokes, but clearly are lying. There are no actual practical joke cases told, though Holmes himself pulls practical jokes on his clients in "The Naval Treaty" and "Mazarin Stone," and he pulls many clever switches on the criminals throughout the series. Of course, in today's society, it's likely students would do something like this to the famous detective.

Sherlock's guesses about "The Hollow Client" include that he was "dressed up in the same fabric as the chair," seen in *A Game of Shadows*.

The Hollow Man is a mystery by John Dickson Carr featuring Doctor Gideon Fell. In 1981, it was selected as the best locked room mystery of all time. There may be an influence here.

The Aluminum Crutch

> This one you'll have read about in the papers. The murder of actor Matthew Michael live on stage. I wasn't actually there as I was on a date (went well, thanks for asking) but Sherlock was and he left a number of messages on my voicemail, telling me what happened. A couple of people have asked me what he's really like so I've transcribed them.
>
> "John, I've just been to see Terror By Night at some terrible little theatre on the Strand. The play itself was mediocre but there was a murder! Live on stage!

What follows is a cozy mystery with the suspects gathering in the drawing room...as a mystery play within an actual cozy mystery. For canon fun, this is one of the lost cases, mentioned in "The Musgrave Ritual." It's also proof that Holmes can be right at *Cluedo* after all...

The Speckled Blonde

Early thirties, dyed blonde hair, strange red speckles all over her body. The woman, Julia Stoner, had been found in her bed. There seemed to be no obvious cause of death. Her sister, Helen, said that Julia had been feeling a bit rundown for the last few weeks but had figured she was stressed because she was getting married soon. It was only after performing the autopsy, that I discovered two tiny puncture marks in her right ankle and traces of an unidentified poison in her bloodstream. The obvious answer was that she had been bitten by something, presumably some kind of snake. As I started to phone the local zoos to see if any had recently escaped, Sherlock looked into Julia's family. She lived with her sister and their stepfather, Doctor Roylott. He was apparently a big name in cosmetics and had even guest starred on Connie Prince's show a few times. Both seemed genuinely devastated by Julia's death. We then met her fiancé, Percy Armitage.

This cast of characters and the situation are basically consistent with "The Speckled Band"...However, the solution lies not in the poisonous snake of the short story, but in another poison altogether. The fiancé is not named in the original, but a fiancé named Percy appears in "The Naval Treaty."

The Geek Interpreter

Chris Melas consults Holmes, insisting the comic book KRATIDES is taking place in real life, with characters like Sophy the Wolflady, The Flying Bludgeon, and Professor Davenport in Beckenham. In the short story "The Greek Interpreter," Mr. Melas is asked to translate for a bandaged prisoner, Mr. Kratides and is taken away down Shaftesbury Avenue by Mr. Latimer, who wields "a most formidable-looking bludgeon." Mr. Kratides's sister Sophie bursts in but is torn away and Melas and Kratides are condemned to death by the villains. In the end, Mr. Davenport offers to solve the mystery of the sad siblings.

Watson and Holmes find themselves in a great comic book battle on Shaftesbury Ave. After the comic book mystery is solved, Watson notes, "They hadn't technically done anything illegal so there wasn't much we could do" (Watson's Blog, "The Geek Interpreter"). He and Holmes face a similar predicament in "A Case of Identity."

The Green Ladder

This case is on Sherlock's blog, written up by him. Thus it lacks the storytelling quality and emotion of John Watson's post, using instead cold analysis for comparison. Holmes narrates two of his original stories and they both come out dry, cold, and unappealing. This feels like notes intended for Sherlock himself rather than a story – appropriate, as this one is drawn from Doyle's own notes. The roughly sketched map mirrors those included in several original tales. As the case begins:

> A PC Jane Downing has come to ask for my help. Her husband died. Everyone thinks it's is so I'm taking on the case.
>> Background: End of last year, Sir Harry Downing died. Left the house to the older son, Jack. House to stay in the family though - it was to go to Keith, the younger brother, if Jack died without having any kids.
>> Last month: Jack found dead in the garden pond. He'd no reason to kill himself but no signs of a struggle. High level of alcohol in his bloodstream. Looks like a tragic accident. Looks like Keith gets the house. (Blog: "The Science of Deduction")

This case is alluded to in "A Study in Pink," as Sherlock borrows Watson's phone to text:

If brother has green ladder
arrest brother.
SH

Holmes notes on his blog:

This is what I do:
1. I observe everything.
2. From what I observe, I deduce everything.
3. When I've eliminated the impossible, whatever remains, no matter how mad it might seem, must be the truth. (Blog: "The Science of Deduction")

This difference between observation and deduction is emphasized in the original series:

"You spoke just now of observation and deduction. Surely the one to some extent implies the other."

"Why, hardly," he answered, leaning back luxuriously in his armchair, and sending up thick blue wreaths from his pipe. "For example, observation shows me that you have been to the Wigmore Street Post-Office this morning, but deduction lets me know that when there you dispatched a telegram."

"Right!" said I. "Right on both points! But I confess that I don't see how you arrived at it. It was a sudden impulse upon my part, and I have mentioned it to no one."

"It is simplicity itself," he remarked, chuckling at my surprise, —"so absurdly simple that an explanation is superfluous; and yet it may serve to define the limits of observation and of deduction. Observation tells me that you have a little reddish mould adhering to your instep….The rest is deduction."

"How, then, did you deduce the telegram?"

"Why, of course I knew that you had not written a letter, since I sat opposite to you all morning. I see also in your open desk there that you have a sheet of stamps and a thick bundle of postcards. What could you go into the post-office for, then, but to send a wire? Eliminate all other factors, and the one which remains must be the truth." ("The Sign of Four")

The Melting Laptop

what happened to the case of the melting laptop?
theimprobableone 16 June 15:23

I'll write it up one day. Thought this [The Geek Interpreter] was more entertaining. – John Watson (Watson's Blog, "The Geek Interpreter")

The Headless Nun

Sherlock's café owner friend Angelo was involved with this one – it likely involved him appearing to throw a drunk Sherlock out of his café. In the unaired pilot, Sherlock requests the same treatment. There appears to have been an actual headless nun (rather than, say, a statue), as Sherlock promises the young boy of "The Sign of Three" a glimpse. "The Headless Monk" was a case in Basil Rathbone's *New Adventures of Sherlock Holmes* radio show of the 1940s. It involves a person masquerading as a headless ghost to capitalize on the local legend.

Diamonds Are Forever

Except they're not. No story here because Sherlock decided not to take the case. Apparently a missing diamond isn't 'interesting' enough. Still, we discovered a body today so that's something for him to get excited about. (Watson's Blog, "Diamonds are Forever")

This case shares names with a James Bond novel. There are several "missing jewel" Holmes cases: "The Sign of Four," "The Adventure of the Blue Carbuncle," "The Adventure of the Beryl Coronet," and "The Adventure of the Mazarin Stone." *Incident at Victoria Falls* also concerns the search for a large diamond.

Murder at "The Orient Express"

When the owner of a Knightsbridge Chinese restaurant was found lying face down in a plate of noodles, Lestrade came to see Sherlock. The man, Terry Wong, had choked to

> death and, at first, it appeared to be an accident. But bruising on Wong's face suggested that he'd been attacked at some point on the evening of his death...after reading about some of the things Wong had done, Sherlock was quite happy to let it go. He was actually impressed by what they'd pulled off. He had an odd sort of justice. For all that he claimed to be cold and uncaring, he had his own sense of right and wrong.

The title obviously nods to Agatha Christie's *Murder on the Orient Express*. Holmes's peculiar justice, including letting criminals escape, appears in "The Adventure of the Devil's Foot," "The Adventure of the Abbey Grange," and "The Adventure of the Blue Carbuncle."

Death by Twitter

> When Ceylan Hassan died, it seemed to be a simple hit-and-run. She'd been to the shops and was crossing the road outside her house when she was hit by a bus. It wasn't nice but it didn't appear to be anything out of the ordinary. Until her brother came to see us, asking us to read her last few tweets. (Watson's Blog, "Death by Twitter").

It's revealed someone's pushing her to commit suicide, something seen (in a sense) in "The Five Orange Pips," among others. The title riffs off the *Death by Chocolate* books among others. This case is also notable because theimprobableone, Sherlock's mysterious fan, ends up helping out.

The Deadly Tealights

> The death of yoga teacher, Tim Leng, was brought to our attention by his flatmate, Scott Bevan. Leng had been found lying, dead, in a bath but he hadn't drowned. He'd been asphyxiated. In a locked room. And we know how much Sherlock likes locked room mysteries.

Sherlock solves it in 36 seconds and Watson gets very defensive about taking long baths. There's also a net troll everyone yells at. The name may riff on the James Bond story *The Living Daylights* or the Turkish baths in the original series.

Tilly Briggs Cruise of Terror

Watson takes this one down, leaving everyone in suspense as his fans gush about how "mindblowing" the case was. The Mathilda Briggs, a ship, is behind the untold tale of the Giant Rat of Sumatra.

Blog Characters

- There are many regular posts on Watson's blog and the few associated ones (Molly and Sherlock have blogs, and there's a tribute to the fallen star of "The Great Game."
- "Met up with Bill Murray. Not the film star. He was the nurse who saved my life when I was shot. He's got married" (Watson's Blog, "Serial Suicides"). Murray is the name of the orderly who saves Watson in the original stories.
- Molly Hooper's blog is pink with kittens.
- Mrs. Hudson confusingly posts as Marie Turner and as herself (suggesting she borrows her neighbor's account but also teasing the book concept where their names are switched.)
- Aside from the obvious characters, there's a more intriguing one:

> of course if i was sherlock's colleague we would have solved the case much earlier. how could you not realise the suitcase would be pink?
> theimprobableone 07 February 15:26
>
> Who the hell are you!??! And what kind of name is that!?!
> Harry Watson 07 February 15:30

i'm an expert on sherlock holmes. i understand him
which is something someone like you would never do.
theimprobableone 07 February 15:32

At least I understand how to use CAPITAL LETTERS!!!!
Harry Watson 07 February 15:43

capital letters are just one of society's conventions that
I choose to ignore. you've just been programmed to be
one of society. you're a sheep. (Watson's Blog, "A
Study in Pink")
theimprobableone 07 February 15:46

Some fans speculate this poster is Sherlock or Mycroft, but
some of the comments point more to an eager fan, a stand-in
for Anderson before Anderson turns fan himself. On Watson's
Blog entry "A Study in Pink," the character gushes, "Oh he's a
genius. I do hope we'll meet one day." Watson actually enlists
this fan's help in his case "Death by Twitter." It's mildly
possible this is Irene Adler, who knows how pink accessories
work and thinks, like theimprobableone, that Sherlock should
find an intellectual equal (though again, the tone seems wrong).

Lost Cases
Archived case files on Sherlock's Blog:
- The Confusion of Isadora Persano (The madness of
  Isadora Persano from a remarkable worm unknown to
  science)
- The Abernetty Family (The lost case of how far the
  parsley sank into the butter)
- The Crooked House (This is an Agatha Christie title)
- The Man With Four Legs (This is a play by Irish author
  Flann O'Brien.)
- The Killer Cats of Greenwich (There's a brute who
  turns a cat loose in an aviary in "The Norwood Builder"
  and a poisonous snake mistaken for a cat in "The
  Speckled Band.")

- The Kirkcudbright Killer (likely a reference to Dorothy L. Sayers' detective story set here)
- The Ghost of St Bartholomew's (This church was used to film the 2009 Sherlock Holmes film. It is supposedly haunted.)
- The Purple Woman (possibly the Perry Mason episode "The Case of the Purple Woman")
- The Laughing Pilot (Christie's *Death in the Clouds*. This could also be "The Case of the Laughing Mummy" from the American 1954 *Sherlock Holmes* television show.)
- The Missing Jars (possibly Agatha Christie's *The Mystery of the Blue Jar*)
- The Invisible Porter ("The Invisible Man," by G. K. Chesterton)
- The Subdivided Crooner (perhaps a search for Elvis)
- The Pale Man (possibly the film *The Case of the Whitechapel Vampire*)
- The Iron Football (possibly Doyle's "The Missing Three-Quarter"). It may also be relevant that in 2010, the filming year, it was finally determined why, in the football game between SMU and TCU, a trophy shaped like an iron skillet is the prize.
- The Major's Cat (possibly Doyle's "The Crooked Man")
- All these of course reflect the enticing unsolved cases mentioned in Holmes canon.

> "Somewhere in the vaults of the bank of Cox and Co., at Charing Cross, there is a travel-worn and battered tin dispatch-box with my name, John H. Watson, M.D., Late Indian Army, painted upon the lid. It is crammed with papers, nearly all of which are records of cases to illustrate the curious problems which Mr. Sherlock Holmes had at various times to examine." ("The Problem of Thor Bridge")

"The idea that Doyle has of coming up with the unrecorded cases, mentioning things you've never seen – brilliant. It's something we've gotten used to, but it's brilliant," Moffat notes (Adams 4).

THE CHARACTERS

Sherlock Holmes

The Profile
Sherlock's profile is particularly iconic from the original stories: Watson notes, "His rooms were brilliantly lit, and, even as I looked up, I saw his tall, spare figure pass twice in a dark silhouette against the blind" ("A Scandal in Bohemia"). They use this profile to catch a killer in "The Adventure of the Empty House." On this show, it appears over and over. It also gets special mention in some of the adaptations. In the parody, *Sherlock Holmes's Smarter Brother*, Holmes is generally only seen in profile. In *The Woman in Green* (1945), Holmes notes that he shares his nose with Julius Caesar. Christopher Lee donned a false nose to play the detective in *Sherlock Holmes and the Deadly Necklace* (1962).

The Actor
Benedict Cumberbatch was cast after Steven Moffat and Mark Gatiss watched his performance in *Atonement* (2007). As part of his preparation, Cumberbatch read every Conan Doyle story.

The Outfit
Mark Gatiss notes:

> In the original stories all it really says is that 'he has a certain quiet primness of dress'; and in the illustrations he wears what an average Victorian man would wear – the

frock coat – and he looks very neat. So that sort of formed the suits, didn't it, with a bit of colour. But the coat is one of those things, and Ray Holman, who was the original costume designer, found this incredible coat. You know it when you see it. He put that little detail of the red buttonhole in, actually – he just sewed that in, which was lovely. But it's a hero coat. ("The Hounds of Baskerville" DVD Commentary)

The Personality
Sherlock begins the series completely unlikeable as he takes Molly for granted, demands irritating favors of Mrs. Hudson and John Watson, and alienates the entire police department. John notes in his blog:

I spoke to a policewoman and she summed Sherlock up. She said "he gets off on it." And he does. He didn't care about the dead woman or any of the other victims. I suspect if he came back and found me and our landlady lying here with our throats cut, he'd just see it as an intellectual exercise. "Fantastic" he'd exclaim, rubbing his hands together. "But the door was locked so how did they kill each other?" (Watson's Blog, "A Study in Pink")

He honestly does come out as a robot as he refuses to eat and notes that "Breathing is boring" in "A Study in Pink." In the first episode, Sherlock is accustomed to being called "Freak," and is genuinely surprised that Watson admires his skills.

"...he had a remarkable gentleness and courtesy in his dealings with women," Watson observes in "The Dying Detective," adding that Holmes "disliked and distrusted the sex, but he was always a chivalrous opponent." At one point Holmes of the books tells a young client he'd hate for his sister to take the position she's been offered, and another time, he comforts a young woman and strokes her hand. Holmes in the 21st century is rarely chivalrous towards Molly, more bluntly callous and cruel. "You say such horrible things," she observes in "A Scandal in Belgravia."

Holmes is downright brutal to Miss Mackenzie, House Mistress of the boarding school as well as the journalist he encounters in "The Reichenbach Fall." The original Holmes didn't walk around London informing people their spouses were cheating on them or that they had terminal illnesses (though House does this with great regularity). He was reasonably polite, accepting that gentlemanly behavior was necessary. Modern Sherlock, by contrast, has clearly decided society's rules are not for him. This, however, gives him the opportunity to grow and change, until he can laugh at himself in his speech at John's wedding.

In "The Great Game," he's awkward about expressing admiration of Watson, but it's clear he feels it. Moriarty correctly notes that Sherlock has a heart (even if he didn't before). At the end of the episode, Sherlock willingly offers his and Watson's life to stop a mass murderer. By "A Scandal in Belgravia," Sherlock appears genuinely vulnerable in his dealings with the sexually experienced Irene Adler. Though he defeats her, he also saves her and appears more sympathetic towards human weakness afterwards:

> And then Sherlock did one of the most human things I think I've ever seen him do – he made Henry look at the dog's body. He didn't need to, he'd solved the case but it was as if he knew that the truly important thing was showing Henry what was real and what wasn't. Maybe the fear and doubt he'd felt, and maybe his experiences with Irene Adler, had humanised him? (Watson's Blog, "The Hounds of Baskerville")

"He does love to be dramatic. Mycroft says" ("A Study in Pink"). This comes straight from the books, not in all the worry about his archnemesis, but in practical jokes and sudden revelations: "Too bad, Lord Cantlemere, too bad!" cries Holmes after slipping the missing gem in their client's pocket. "My old friend here will tell you that I have an impish habit of practical joking. Also that I can never resist a dramatic situation" ("The Adventure of the Mazarin Stone"). Sherlock certainly has a sense of humor on the show, as he jokes with Watson and grins as he reveals that the secretary's been wearing a pin worth nine million pounds.

> A flush of colour sprang to Holmes's pale cheeks, and he bowed to us like the master dramatist who receives the homage of his audience. It was at such moments that for an instant he ceased to be a reasoning machine, and betrayed his human love for admiration and applause. The same singularly proud and reserved nature which turned away with disdain from popular notoriety was capable of being moved to its depths by spontaneous wonder and praise from a friend. ("The Six Napoleons")

In "The Reichenbach Fall," it's revealed how much the police truly despise him for his arrogant cleverness. By episode end, however, Sherlock proves he truly is a part of society. Sherlock offers his life to protect Watson and his other loved ones, proving that he isn't nearly so isolated as he wants others to believe. It's Moriarty who has no one, who knows his life is worth nothing, money is worth nothing, nothing matters except (like Sherlock) finding a relief from his boredom.

On his return from death, Sherlock appears ignorant of how devastatingly he wounded his friend. However, he has grown kinder. Unlike Holmes's cruel deductions on Molly's love life in "A Study in Pink" and "A Scandal in Belgravia," Sherlock begins the third season deciding not to comment on Molly's newest man or identify Mary as being a liar. At John's wedding, he teams up with bridesmaid Janine and volunteers his skills to find her a good man.

Saying he doesn't need people would be inaccurate – he appears to want to control every situation, so he likes people around when they're helpful and predictable. Watson mentions this to Lestrade in "The Hounds of Baskerville":

> JOHN: You know he's actually pleased you're here?
> (Greg throws him a disbelieving look.)
> JOHN: *Secretly* pleased.
> LESTRADE: Is he? That's nice. I suppose he likes having all the same faces back together. Appeals to his...his...
> JOHN:...Asperger's? [This is a mild type of autism in which people frequently become strongly focused on hobbies or interests.]

John, who is an actual doctor with some experience at psychotherapy is providing a far more accurate diagnosis than Sherlock does – Sherlock is not a sociopath (who would be incapable of feeling the emotions at all) but autistic, with trouble relating to people. It seems likely that Sherlock has found a convenient label for himself (that he can use as an insult before others do). Deciding he's a sociopath frees him from much responsibility of trying to relate to others, incorrect though his diagnosis is.

John H. Watson

"Perhaps I'll write about some of the other mundane stuff I do like playing board games or eating sandwiches and drinking tea in front of the *Eastenders!*" (Watson's Blog, "The Sign of Three"). Watson is of course the everyman. He's also, as in the books, Sherlock's narrator and interpreter. He apologizes for his friend and tries to coach him in proper behavior. As Sherlock concentrates on the problem, John clings to the human element: "It makes me furious to think about those poor people who got into his taxi - one of them was just a kid! They must have gone through hell" (Watson's Blog, "A Study in Pink").

When Gatiss asks Martin Freeman about his choice of clothes for John, Freeman notes, "I was trying to have a nod towards his twin careers or twin professions of medicine and army and thought that there was a 'pukka'-ness to them both traditionally." He felt that there might be other army doctors in the family and "it's just a certain understated English style" with functional utilitarian-style gear. "It's relaxed/informal but never less than smart," agrees Mark. Martin continues, "Being an army officer and a doctor are both fairly – for want of a *much* better word – quite posh professions. I don't think John is ultra-posh, but he's just proper and quietly stylish" ("The Great Game" DVD Commentary)

Steven Moffat says that Martin is "the sort of opposite of Benedict in everything except the amount of talent. Benedict is a magnificent exotic animal as an actor, isn't he? He doesn't look like a normal person; he rarely plays normal people. He plays exceptional people. But Martin finds a sort of poetry in the ordinary man. I love the fastidious realism of everything he does" ("A Study in Pink" DVD Commentary). Martin Freeman notes:

> John is...in a way he's like Sherlock's kind of moral compass, because Sherlock's mind is so genuinely brilliant, he doesn't always stop to consider the whys and wherefores or the rights or wrongs of what is, and John is kind of like his moral barometer there. And he's a more *decent* person, in a way, than Sherlock, because he's more normal, you know. Sherlock is genuinely extraordinary. ("Unlocking Sherlock")

He makes a perfect sidekick for Holmes, willingly dropping everything to follow him around London on cases. His job, as it does in the book series, fades away to nearly unimportant beside Sherlock's cases – When Sherlock returns in "The Empty Hearse," he's genuinely surprised that John's moved on in his life.

John takes charge on occasion, grappling with Moriarty to save Sherlock's life in "The Great Game." Sherlock may have medical knowledge, but he lacks the practical – with an injured man present, Watson springs to take charge and makes Sherlock be his "nurse" ("The Sign of Three"). Sherlock notes in his speech at John's wedding:

> There was one feature, and only one feature of interest, in the whole of this baffling case. And quite frankly it was the usual. John Watson. Who while I was trying to solve a murder, instead saved a life. There are mysteries worth solving and stories worth telling. The best and bravest man I know, on top of that he actually knows how to do stuff. Except wedding planning and serviettes, he's rubbish at those...But a word to the wise. Should any of you require the services of either of us, I will solve your murder. But it takes John Watson to save your life. ("The Sign of Three")

"His Last Vow" emphasizes Watson's violent toughness. "I'm a doctor – I know how to sprain people," he says after getting rough with a knife and tire iron. Sherlock points out that as much as John may think he craves normalcy, he truly wants the war he left behind...that's how he chose his wife.

Mycroft Holmes

Mycroft appears in only two of the original cases – he also helps Sherlock with his faked death and reappearance from behind the scenes. He first appears in "The Greek Interpreter":

> Mycroft Holmes was a much larger and stouter man than Sherlock. His body was absolutely corpulent, but his face, though massive, had preserved something of the sharpness of expression which was so remarkable in that of his brother. His eyes, which were of a peculiarly light, watery gray, seemed to always retain that far-away, introspective look which I had only observed in Sherlock's when he was exerting his full powers.
>
> "I am glad to meet you, sir," said he, putting out a broad, fat hand like the flipper of a seal. "I hear of Sherlock everywhere since you became his chronicler. By the way, Sherlock, I expected to see you round last week, to consult me over that Manor House case. I thought you might be a little out of your depth."

In the books, therefore, he is admiring of Watson – the source of Sherlock's fame. He is presented as Sherlock's intellectual superior, but also as a man who lacks any energy – as Sherlock puts it, "he has no ambition and no energy. He will not even go out of his way to verify his own solution, and would rather be considered wrong than take the trouble to prove himself right." Sherlock often comes to him with cases that require a bit of outside advice, just as the police do with him.

On the show, Mycroft is possibly the slimmest he's ever been in adaptations, though jokes are made about his yo-yoing weight. In "The Sign of Three," we see him exercising, and Sherlock suggests that this is something he does regularly.

> As Mycroft arrives, Mark jokes, "The original dialogue here was that John Watson says, 'Who is that beautiful man?'" "But then we cast it!" adds Steven, joking, "When that actor failed to show up, [we said,] 'Mark, would you mind popping on?'" "Get the suit on," says Mark, then continues, "We made this decision that Mycroft would have a yo-yoing

weight problem. It gives me freedom between (hopeful) seasons to let myself go." ("A Study in Pink" DVD Commentary)

In both stories, the two brothers are less-than-warm – Both are likely to use the other for their professional skills and abilities rather than a social get-together. Mycroft on the show mocks Sherlock for calling on Christmas, and is horrified at taking their parents to the theater. This brittle relationship is very much seen in *The Private Life of Sherlock Holmes,* which the creators cite as an enormous influence on their Mycroft.

The massive joke in the first episode is that Mycroft appears to be Moriarty – his slimness, secretiveness and power, covert interest in Sherlock all hint at darker matters. Then there's his sinister introduction of himself:

JOHN: Who *are* you?
M: An interested party.
JOHN: Interested in Sherlock? Why? I'm guessing you're not friends.
M: You've met him. How many 'friends' do you imagine he has? I am the closest thing to a friend that Sherlock Holmes is capable of having.
JOHN: And what's that?
M: An enemy.
JOHN: An enemy?
M: In his mind, certainly. If you were to ask him, he'd probably say his arch-enemy. He does love to be dramatic. (John looks pointedly around the warehouse.)
JOHN (sarcastically): Well, thank God you're above all that. ("A Study in Pink")

Watson is relieved at episode end to discover Mycroft's interest in Sherlock Holmes actually is caring and concerned rather than malicious.

MOFFAT: I think we have to 'fess up that our interpretation of Mycroft is probably not Doyle's at all but Billy Wilder's.
GATISS: Apart from the Rathbone films, our favourite really is the Billy Wilder film *The Private Life of Sherlock Holmes* – a very underrated film which I think now is much more appreciated. ("A Study in Pink" DVD Commentary)

Mycroft's covert government plots in *The Private Life of Sherlock Holmes* and his mixture of censure and sympathy for Sherlock's infatuation with a foreign spy all are repeated in "A Scandal in Belgravia."

Jim Moriarty

> My nerves are fairly proof, Watson, but I must confess to a start when I saw the very man who had been so much in my thoughts standing there on my threshold. His appearance was quite familiar to me. He is extremely tall and thin, his forehead domes out in a white curve, and his two eyes are deeply sunken in his head. He is clean-shaven, pale, and ascetic-looking, retaining something of the professor in his features. His shoulders are rounded from much study, and his face protrudes forward, and is forever slowly oscillating from side to side in a curiously reptilian fashion. He peered at me with great curiosity in his puckered eyes. ("The Final Problem")

Holmes's nemesis is mentioned in seven of the original sixty cases, though it's rare to see a movie without him. He is the ultimate villain, the only one capable of defeating Sherlock Holmes, as Data remarks when accidently creating a Moriarty to be his nemesis on *Star Trek: The Next Generation*. Thus, fans recognized him in the schemes of this show's Mycroft, long before Moriarty's first appearance.

In the books, he's best known for his absence, as he doesn't act himself, only organizes crimes. Holmes explains:

> For years past I have continually been conscious of some power behind the malefactor, some deep organizing power which forever stands in the way of the law, and throws its shield over the wrong-doer. Again and again in cases of the most varying sorts – forgery cases, robberies, murders – I have felt the presence of this force, and I have deduced its action in many of those undiscovered crimes in which I have not been personally consulted. For years I have endeavored to break through the veil which shrouded it, and at last the time came when I seized my thread and followed it, until it led me, after a thousand cunning

windings, to ex-Professor Moriarty of mathematical celebrity.

He is the Napoleon of crime, Watson. He is the organizer of half that is evil and of nearly all that is undetected in this great city. He is a genius, a philosopher, an abstract thinker. He has a brain of the first order. He sits motionless, like a spider in the center of its web, but that web has a thousand radiations, and he knows well every quiver of each of them. He does little himself. He only plans. But his agents are numerous and splendidly organized. ("The Final Problem")

Thus the first series is marked by two of Moriarty's henchmen, then many people forced to pass on the archvillain's quips before he appears in person to menace Sherlock face to face. (*Elementary* takes a similar approach, with a man who typically stands in for Moriarty over the phone.) When "Jim" Moriarty [Andrew Scott] finally appears in his own person, he's quirky, playful, and utterly mad, a new interpretation unlike many of his predecessors onscreen. Mark Gatiss explains:

Andrew came in to read for this part and everybody just really fell for his interpretation. The thing about Moriarty – obviously as with the reinterpretation of Sherlock and John – he was never gonna be a sixty year old bald professor. He was going to be something else, and something hiding in plain sight, as it were. And we saw a lot of great people, but what Andrew brought to it immediately was a kind of playful super-intensity; and for all the sort of camp fun of some of these lines, which are demanded by a Holmes and Moriarty confrontation, there are moments in it which are so scary, I think, when his face becomes a lizard-like set mask and this real evil just comes through, I think is really remarkable. ("The Great Game" DVD Commentary)

There are other attempts to make this Moriarty unique – the original was arrogant, nearly godlike, rather than this young figure who teases Sherlock like a school chum. He can get away with wearing a grey suit and cream tie rather than menacing black. Nonetheless, his pure desperation for revenge against Holmes and his allies comes straight from the books, as do other qualities. Gatiss notes:

> There's two little things here: "Moriarty" is an Irish name and there's never been an Irish Moriarty, so we actually asked Andrew to do it in his own accent...One of the little details in the original story is that Moriarty's head is forever oscillating from side to side in a curiously reptilian fashion. And I told Andrew that on the costume fitting and he didn't know, and absolutely grabbed it, and I saw him, literally as he was going, he was just practicing it for the first time, and he just pops it in every now and then, particularly at the end. ("The Great Game" DVD Commentary)

Scott notes, "The reaction to Moriarty has been incredible. I couldn't be more happy and more proud to be in the show. It's very difficult to find a popular and clever show" (Jeffery and Mansell). Asked if the villain could have somehow survived, Scott told interviewers: "That's an impossible question to answer! It's very hard to come back from shooting yourself in the mouth, we all know that" (Jeffery and Mansell).

Moriarty appears to be dead at the end of series two, but the cleverest, wealthiest criminal in the world likely has a way around this if desired. Series three leaves viewers uncertain, with another year of speculation ready to go. In the Rathbourne films, he returns from death, and Moran (not yet used on the show) appears as well. Further, in various levels of canon, Moriarty has brothers, and in some adaptations, they take his place or take over for him. The producers have said they plan to focus on Holmes's other great enemies (of which there are plenty), but Moriarty still has possibilities remaining.

Charles Augustus Magnussen

> Charles Augustus Milverton was a man of fifty, with a large, intellectual head, a round, plump, hairless face, a perpetual frozen smile, and two keen grey eyes, which gleamed brightly from behind broad, golden-rimmed glasses. There was something of Mr. Pickwick's benevolence in his appearance, marred only by the insincerity of the fixed smile and by the hard glitter of those restless and penetrating eyes. His voice was as smooth and suave as

his countenance, as he advanced with a plump little hand extended, murmuring his regret for having missed us at his first visit. Holmes disregarded the outstretched hand and looked at him with a face of granite. Milverton's smile broadened; he shrugged his shoulders, removed his overcoat, folded it with great deliberation over the back of a chair, and then took a seat. ("The Adventure of Charles Augustus Milverton")

Any villain following Moriarty certainly has a difficult task. Charles Augustus Magnussen manages it by being utterly repellent, attacking all that is decent and good in the world with a nasty sliminess. Moffat notes that Andrew Scott's Moriarty is "such an act to follow." "We needed an utterly terrifying villain and Lars just scares...you the moment he shows up!" said the writer (Jeffrey). He enjoys owning people, as the worst sort of bully, one completely unchecked by kindness or reason. With his inner knowledge of people, he emphasizes who Sherlock could be if he gave up on morality – as it turns out, the evil Magnussen brings out a great heroism in the Great Detective.

"We had a notion that maybe he might be American and at that point we kept the original name," Moffat explained. "It was actually [producer] Sue [Vertue] who originally suggested that we have a look at Lars. I then went onto a website and looked up all the Danish names that sounded a bit like 'Milverton' and came up with Magnussen!" (Jeffery)

Mary Morstan

In books and show, Mary urges Watson to keep doing cases with Holmes because Watson enjoys them so much. While she loves John, she's willing to share him, and she understands his need for excitement...more than he could ever guess. Book Mary was supportive but always stayed behind. Show Mary never hesitates for a moment.

On the show, she's a smarter Watson, assisting Holmes and quickly discovering the right answer. In the book, Holmes gives her high praise. "I think she is one of the most charming young ladies I ever met, and might have been most useful in such work as we have been doing. She had a decided genius that way: witness the way in which she preserved that Agra plan from all the other papers of her father" ("The Sign of the Four").

In the books, she meets Watson on a case in September of 1888, while seeking the Agra treasure, for which her father left her a map. However, another wife is mentioned after Mary dies (in the three-year gap of Holmes's death). There may even be a third wife, according to the dates. Of course, Doyle was often inconsistent, so fans attempts to organize Sherlock's life, however clever, must occasionally end in conundrums.

On the show, Mary's cleverness and her past may make her a welcome addition to the team in season four – while Sherlock provides the analysis, and John the courage and humanity, Mary's own perfect memory and other skills will prove an asset on their future adventures, though an unusual mix in the famous duo.

Mrs. Hudson

> Mrs. Hudson, the landlady of Sherlock Holmes, was a long-suffering woman. Not only was her first-floor flat invaded at all hours by throngs of singular and often undesirable characters but her remarkable lodger showed an eccentricity and irregularity in his life which must have sorely tried her patience....The landlady stood in the deepest awe of him and never dared to interfere with him, however outrageous his proceedings might seem. She was fond of him, too, for he had a remarkable gentleness and courtesy in his dealings with women. ("The Adventure of the Dying Detective")

The irreverent lady once married to a mobster, whose slogan is "I'm not your housekeeper" seems a complete subversion of the original character. Mrs. Hudson is mostly seen silently opening the door or bringing tea when clients arrive – she rarely offers opinions. She's always present in the movies, but frequently does little besides opening the door, pouring the tea, and making a motherly fuss over the state of the rooms.

A notable aspect of her character is her relationship with the friendless Holmes. When Mrs. Hudson is attacked in "The Reichenbach Fall," Sherlock shows his devotion, both through his memorable line "Mrs. Hudson leave Baker Street? England would fall" and with his vicious retribution against the man who tortured her. Sherlock's famed chivalry may mostly have vanished, but it's still present in this single scene.

> GATISS: It's such a wonderful warm relationship. Mrs Hudson in the stories really is just a mention. Over the years in different versions, she's generally a sort of Mrs Pepperpot figure because Holmes and Watson are usually much older, but it's so nice to have that kind of maternal feeling there in the household.
> MOFFAT: Well that's where it came from, really. Even if you read the script of A Study in Pink, there's no real indication of that at all. It was just Benedict giving her hugs and kisses all the time 'cause it was Una, so we just started writing it in there. (Commentary, "A Scandal in Belgravia")

Of course, Mrs. Hudson is no stranger to violent crime, as she relates her sinister past to John before his wedding:

> JOHN: Did you think you'd found the right one when you married Mr. Hudson?
> MRS HUDSON (smiling): No! It was just a whirlwind thing for us. I knew it wouldn't work, but I just got sort of swept along.
> JOHN: Right.
> MRS HUDSON: And then we moved to Florida. We had a fantastic time, but of course I didn't know what he was up to. (Whispering) The drugs.
> JOHN (laughing): Drugs? (He grimaces at the pain in his head.)
> MRS HUDSON: He was running...um, oh God, what d'you call it? Um, a...cartel.
> (John props his head up with his fingers.)
> MRS HUDSON: Got in with a really bad crowd.
> JOHN: Right.
> MRS HUDSON: And then I found out about all the other women. I didn't have a clue! So, when he was actually arrested for blowing someone's head off...
> (John's eyes drift sideways, perhaps a little confused by the

matter-of-fact way she just said the phrase.)
MRS HUDSON:...it was quite a relief, to be honest.

She appears to take some illegal substance for her hip, as she reveals in the first episode. She protests she was "just typing" for the drug cartel in "His Last Vow," but has trouble explaining away the "exotic dancing."

Sherlock is not always kind to her – he often dismisses and uses her much as he does Molly Hooper. In "The Great Game," she tries to explain her difficulty in renting 221C, but Sherlock cuts her off midsentence with a closed door. Her wounded expression, like Molly's on many occasions, emphasizes her hurt at this sort of treatment.

Her rallying cry of "not your housekeeper" is a sly nod to one of Conan Doyle's confusing potential inconsistencies. In "A Study in Scarlet," she is presented as the landlady, while in later stories, she's the housekeeper – answering the door and bringing their meals on order. Of course, on the show, she acts much like their mother – objecting to the property damage but still always awaiting them at home with food and a comforting ear.

Molly Hooper

Strangely, there are no Mollys or Hoopers in all of Holmes canon – she really is an original character, rather than a distant adaptation of another character. Like the rare original characters in other book-to-show adaptations like *A Game of Thrones,* her character has an unknown fate – fans of the books knew Sherlock would come back from his Reichenbach Fall as he did in the books, but anything could happen to Molly. This adds uncertainty and even mystery to her character.

Molly is in the sad position of being used by Sherlock and taken for granted. While she clearly has a crush on him (or more) in the first two years of the show, he's generally only polite to her when seeking a favor. She in turn appears willing to take his abuse and still bring him coffee, wheel out bodies, or whatever he wishes. As a critic comments, "The pining, put-upon character of Molly Hooper in *Sherlock,* one of the few characters with no easy equivalent in the original stories, is painful to watch as she mopes around after Holmes like a lovesick puppy. A lot of fanfic sets out to put that right, ensuring that Molly gets the boy, her own adventure, revenge, or all three" (Penny).

On her blog, she takes a moment to express her feelings firsthand:

> Do you believe in love at first sight? There's this man and I love him. At least, I think I do. I can't stop thinking about him. He's so intelligent it's like he's burning. And he's so cool but not really. And he's fit. Oh, he is really fit. And I can't stop thinking about him. (Molly Hooper's Blog)

She does however realize that he's using her, especially in "The Blind Banker":

> "Oh, and Sherlock came in again tonight. And he was his usual arrogant self! And he was blatantly flirting with me and I know he's doing it and I should tell him to stop but I don't! And, of course, he was only doing it so I'd help him with something. As soon as he got what he wanted, he was off." (Molly Hooper's Blog)

In canon, Sherlock Holmes used another young woman terribly as a tool, playing with her emotions regardless of her trampled feelings. This was Agatha, housemaid to the vicious blackmailer Charles Augustus Milverton. He goes on walks with her disguised as a plumber, and as their relationship progresses, he proposes marriage and she accepts.

> "I wanted information, Watson."
> "Surely you have gone too far?"
> "It was a most necessary step."
> ...
> "But the girl, Holmes?"
> He shrugged his shoulders.
> "You can't help it, my dear Watson. You must play your cards as best you can when such a stake is on the table."

His callous dismissal of her feelings as collateral damage emphasizes that even original Holmes is not always as chivalrous and kind as he appears. Of course, this scene is revisited in "His Last Vow."

At the Christmas party of "A Scandal in Belgravia," Sherlock tramples Molly's feelings more cruelly and publicly than ever before, and chagrined, makes an apology:

> I see you've got a new boyfriend, Molly, and you're serious about him...Oh, come on. Surely you've all seen the present at the top of the bag – perfectly wrapped with a bow. All the others are slapdash at best. It's for someone special, then. The shade of red echoes her lipstick – either an unconscious association or one that she's deliberately trying to encourage. Either way, Miss Hooper has lurrrve on her mind. The fact that she's serious about him is clear from the fact she's giving him a gift at all. That would suggest long-term hopes, however forlorn; and that she's seeing him tonight is evident from her make-up and what she's wearing.

When he discovers the present is for him, he looks stricken and says, "I am sorry. Forgive me." He kisses her cheek. "Merry Christmas, Molly Hooper." Benedict Cumberbatch notes: "It's one of those moments which I love because he's trying to do the right thing in a way, but also he's just flaring up because he can't stand the usual niceties of Christmas; and it's a part of the episode where all empathy for him goes out of the window. He really is on full throttle, so he's outplayed through his cruelty." (Commentary, "A Scandal in Belgravia")

Of course, this moment is spoiled by a gift from Irene Adler, a sudden reminder that the Holmes who could love Molly Hooper is far far outside canon. His ideal mate is Irene Adler or someone like her – his intellectual equal (or superior!). *The Private Life of Sherlock Holmes* or *Sherlock Holmes and the Leading Lady* are both in-character romances – in both, Sherlock appears aware of the woman's charms, but spends his time matching wits with the international spy and femme fatale rather than straying into romance. The Robert Downey Jr. movie, with Sherlock as action hero after a torrid affair with Irene Adler is more out of character.

173

Molly is invaluable to Sherlock in faking his death – not only searching all of London for the body he requires but also keeping his secret for years. When Sherlock returns, he attempts to thank her with the greatest gift he feels he can give – a chance to join him for what gives him the most pleasure:

> SHERLOCK: Molly?
> MOLLY: Yes?
> SHERLOCK: Would you...
> (He stops, looking down, then slowly starts to walk closer.)
> SHERLOCK: Would you like to...
> MOLLY:...have dinner?
> SHERLOCK (simultaneously):...solve crimes?
> MOLLY (awkwardly): Ooh. ("The Empty Hearse")

In this activity, she proves able, but not a perfect substitute for Watson, the partnership Sherlock truly craves. "It was a real honour to spend a day helping Sherlock. I'm not John though," Molly notes (Watson's Blog, "The Empty Hearse"). At episode end, it's revealed that Molly has moved on and gotten engaged...to someone who strongly resembles Sherlock! It seems Molly hasn't grown as much as she pretends. Sherlock however has become kind enough not to mention this. Her relationship with Tom continues through the next episode:

> SHERLOCK: You look...well.
> MOLLY: I am.
> SHERLOCK: How's...Tom?
> MOLLY: Not a sociopath.
> SHERLOCK: Still good.
> MOLLY: And we're having quite a lot of sex.
> SHERLOCK: Okaaay. ("The Sign of Three")

Molly is in a far healthier relationship – she has everything Sherlock couldn't give her. Nonetheless, Tom proves he's not very insightful during Sherlock's mystery speech at the wedding. Sadly, things appear to go badly by "His Last Vow," so perhaps Sally realizes she isn't truly in love with him.

Greg Lestrade

Lestrade's first name, Greg, is a nod to Inspector Gregson – these are the two most commonly appearing detectives from the books.

> Lestrade doesn't appear all that often in the novels and is quite inconsistent in them. Mark and Steven decided to go with the version who appeared in The Six Napoleons: he's a man who is frustrated by Holmes but admires him, and who Holmes considers as the best person at Scotland Yard, "and actually," says Gatiss, "if Sherlock Holmes wasn't around, you'd like Greg Lestrade on your case, I think." ("A Study in Pink" DVD Commentary)

Lestrade of "The Adventure of the Six Napoleons" is quite admiring of Sherlock, even gushing. The case involves the odd occurrence of a man smashing Napoleon busts, and soon a grisly murder as well. Lestrade solves the murder through conventional detective work, and Holmes is admiring in his praise. However, Lestrade dismisses the busts as unimportant, until Sherlock manages to prove they're the crux of the case. Sherlock frequently mentions that the Scotland Yard detectives have energy, persistence, bravery, and many other fine qualities, lacking only imagination is cases such as this. Lestrade's final speech is unusually generous, and reflects an attitude about his fellow police that is not typically seen in either show or books.

> "Well," said Lestrade, "I've seen you handle a good many cases, Mr. Holmes, but I don't know that I ever knew a more workmanlike one than that. We're not jealous of you at Scotland Yard. No, sir, we are very proud of you, and if you come down to-morrow there's not a man, from the oldest inspector to the youngest constable, who wouldn't be glad to shake you by the hand." ("The Six Napoleons")

In the books, he and the other inspectors have little personality outside the job. On the show, Greg Lestrade has been fleshed out a bit. In his personal life, he has an unhappy relationship with his wife, who cheats on him. He's seen drinking heavily at John and Mary's wedding, perhaps thinking of his own unhappy one. Like Sherlock himself, he is often alone, without the lover or best friend who can complete him. Nonetheless, he seems to take a paternal interest in Sherlock as well as a professional one.

They saw several actors who auditioned for Lestrade but all of them came across as slightly comic, whereas "with Rupert," says Moffat, "you thought he could have his own series being Lestrade. It's like, if Sherlock Holmes doesn't turn up, there is another television series where Inspector Lestrade solves the crime!" Moffat adds, "he seems like a handsome man but no-one's told him, 'You're actually terribly good looking'. There's also something very fatherly about Rupert. The fact that he's got four children probably helps!" ("A Study in Pink" DVD Commentary)

Sherlock in turn seems to prefer him to any other detective – at the beginning of the first episode, Lestrade appears to be the only one willing to work with Sherlock. Gregson in *Elementary* has a similar relationship with the detective – both appear to be Sherlock's closest acquaintance before Watson arrives on the scene.

JUST FOR THE AUDIENCE

Fun with the Fourth Wall

Most notably, Sherlock's website and John's blog make their world come alive. Molly Hooper has her own blog, and there's a fansite for the dead celebrity from "The Great Game." "Neither me or Sherlock have Twitter accounts (all those accounts are fake)," Watson notes, reminding visitors that only his blog is real (Watson's Blog, "Death by Twitter"). The fourth wall seems to tremble and nearly break when a character posts:

> Wait are any of you real? Is any of this real? How do we know that people like "Harry Watson" and "Mike Stamford" aren't just made up for this blog? – TheRealJoe (Watson's Blog, Murder at 'The Orient Express')

Well, I'm glad that our purpose here is to entertain people. There was me thinking we were solving crimes," Sherlock posts sarcastically. (Watson's Blog, "The Geek Interpreter"). On another occasion, he notes:

> John, this is appalling. It's all 'and then we ran here! And then we ran there! And it was a code!' What about the analysis, John? The analysis! How did I work it out? How did I know where to go? And as for 'All these people he involves in his adventures...'. My what? I'm sorry, obviously

I didn't realize I was a character in a children's story.
(Watson's Blog, "The Blind Banker)

The unseen cases Sherlock lists on his site involve a murder-mystery play with a real murder inside it, solved by the "real" Sherlock Holmes and a story of comic book characters coming to life. Holmes and Watson must pretend to be more of those characters, and the story ends with an offer to put Holmes and Watson in comics. The mind is lost in circles. At the close of their adventures, Chris Melas plans to make a graphic novel series based on Sherlock Holmes (Watson's Blog, "The Geek Interpreter")...of course, these already exist.

It's also amusing that Watson has two cases he chooses not to post about – in the original series, he teases readers with many cases that are too controversial or horrific to set in words, such as "the giant rat of Sumatra, a story for which the world is not yet prepared" ("The Adventure of the Sussex Vampire").

Really, John, what's the point in this post? If you can't detail what happened in a case because of some ridiculous law thing then why bother?
Sherlock Holmes

It adds context. Gives people an idea about the real you.
John Watson

How does it? And why should people want to know the real me? What's the point?!
Sherlock Holmes (Watson's Blog, "The Woman")

Of course, in his wedding toast, Sherlock becomes the narrator (as John is on the blog and during "The Reichenbach Fall" as he bookends the story with his own reactions). He also describes what he calls "our frankly ridiculous adventures." As he adds, "From now on, there's a new story. A better adventure," Sherlock adds. It seems he's not only willing to indulge his fandom, but to turn from fictional character to storyteller as well.

At the end of "His Last Vow," the music of the credits start, and Lestrade is seen in a bar where men shout "There's something wrong with the telly!" It does feel as if viewers' sets have been taken over, as well as those onscreen, as a familiar face makes an appearance. A meme going around just after the episode aired pointed out that the British people are so polite that they announce when there will be a scene after the credits.

Sherlock's Fandom

"Anyway, time to go and be Sherlock Holmes," Sherlock notes, then dons the famous hat with resignation ("The Empty Hearse"). He leaves his home to meet the reporters and give an interview...much as Benedict Cumberbatch must do on a daily basis. Sherlock becomes an "Internet Phenomenon" with slogans like "Hat Man and Robin" after he puts on the deerstalker. ("A Scandal in Belgravia"). Around the same time in real life (after series one), the show likewise became such an internet sensation. Thus as Sherlock Holmes's fans grow increasingly eager, they resemble real-life fans of *Sherlock*.

It must also be mentioned that Gatiss and Moffat have described themselves of two of the biggest fans of all time, obsessively pouring over the stories and movies. As they gush:

> MOFFAT: Oh, God, yes! Mark and I are absolute fanboys of Sherlock Holmes.
> GATISS: I read The Adventures first and then I got the Complete Sherlock Holmes...
> RUSSEL TOVEY: What age was this?
> GATISS: Oh, eight or nine; and I read 'em all because I wanted to be able to say I had read all of Sherlock Holmes – and as Steven pointed out, 'Only an idiot geek would think that would somehow make me cool'! ("The Hounds of Baskerville" DVD Commentary)

Having fans create these overwhelmingly established franchises (*Doctor Who* as well as *Sherlock*) is a dream come alive for fans, as they watch enormous fans create the franchises they grew up with. "What *Doctor Who* and *Sherlock* offer us right now is a chance to see what modern fan fiction would look like if it was written by well-paid, well-respected middle-aged men with a big fat budget. That sort of fanfiction is usually referred to simply as 'fiction'," notes one amused critic (Penny).

John's blog is one particular place where fannishness runs rampant, as fictional characters post about how much they enjoy their hatted hero. At Christmas, Sherlock complains about John's blog:

> SHERLOCK: You've got a photograph of me wearing that hat?!
> JOHN: People like that hat.
> SHERLOCK: No they don't, what people?

"I held my breath for what seemed like months," John writes on his blog, mirroring fans' months-long wait for the conclusion to "The Reichenbach Fall."

Of course, Anderson and his club of The Empty Hearse are the most fannish of all. As Anderson puts it, "I founded 'The Empty Hearse' so like-minded people could meet, discuss theories..." They meet in a decorated room, dressed in Sherlock hats and scarves, to discuss the deeper meanings behind their hero's actions and make predictions about his future – just like television fan clubs. They offer several theories on how Sherlock may have escaped death, all of them popular ones fans posted on the internet in the intervening year. In the midst of the meeting, Twitter goes mad with the messages fans were posting all year in real life – #SherlockHolmesAlive!, #SherlockLives, and #SherlockIsNotDead.

The dream-scenario in which Sherlock and Moriarty are actually lovers playing a trick on Watson seems like fanfiction brought to life in a clever wave at viewers. The teenage member of their conspiracy club points out her interpretation is hardly less fanciful than anything anyone else has come up with.

At last, Sherlock confides the (possibly true) story of how he escaped death not to his best friends, but to the fan club, much as if he's directly telling the watchers. Anderson, like all fans, immediately starts poking holes.

> SHERLOCK: Neat, don't you think?
> ANDERSON: Hmm.

SHERLOCK: What?
(Anderson shrugs.)
ANDERSON: Not the way I'd have done it.
SHERLOCK (folding his arms): Oh really?
ANDERSON: No, I'm not saying it's not clever, but...
SHERLOCK: What?
ANDERSON:...Bit...disappointed.
(Sherlock sighs.)
SHERLOCK: Everyone's a critic. ("The Empty Hearse")

"The Empty Hearse" has other moments as Sherlock and his friends seem to acknowledge a large audience presence: John for instance must shave his mustache because "everyone hates it" – suggesting viewers as well as his friends.

JOHN: I don't shave for Sherlock Holmes.
MARY: Oh! You should put that on a T-shirt!

Undoubtedly, it will be one soon. There's also

JOHN: I don't understand.
MAGNUSSEN: You should get that on a t-shirt.
...
JOHN: But I still don't understand.
MAGNUSSEN: And that's the back of the t-shirt.

JOHN: You'd have to be an idiot not to see it. You love it.
SHERLOCK (turning to face him): Love what?
JOHN: Being Sherlock Holmes.

While Cumberbatch may find the media attention increasingly heavy, he does seem to love his role.

"His Last Vow" sees Mycroft actually employing Sherlock's fanclub, as the only ones who might be willing to explore his filthy rooms. Later, it is announced that Sherlock cannot be incarcerated in any prison without inciting riots on a daily basis, presumably from a country of eager fans.

There are smaller fannish moments as well:

Moriarty is introduced in the first episode as Holmes's "fan."

"That's the frailty of genius, John: it needs an audience,"

Sherlock notes ("A Study in Pink").

- In "A Scandal in Belgravia," John could be addressing the show's fandom itself when he says, "Who the hell knows about Sherlock Holmes, but for the record – if anyone out there still cares – I'm not actually gay."

- Sherlock composes theme music for Irene Adler, throughout "A Scandal in Belgravia"...apparently, he's *her* fan.

- The prison's governor in "The Reichenbach Fall" has a "Keep calm and carry on" mug. Most fan conventions sell mugs and shirts like these, complete with twists on the catchphrase straight from *Harry Potter, Doctor Who,* and *Sherlock* itself. These include "Keep Calm and Shoot the Wall" (complete with smiley face), "Keep Calm and Text Sherlock," "Keep Calm and Go to Your Mind Palace," "Keep Calm: It's an Experiment," and even "Keep Calm and Hold Hands with your Favorite Sociopath."

- The reporter in "The Reichenbach Fall" dresses as Sherlock's fangirl, wearing a deerstalker and fan button.

- Sherlock, of course, doesn't understand fannish behavior:

> JOHN: People want to know you're human.
> SHERLOCK: Why?
> JOHN: 'Cause they're interested.
> SHERLOCK: No they're not. *Why* are they? ("A Scandal in Belgravia.")

CONCLUSION

Moffat and Gatiss are in no hurry to make a *Sherlock* movie, as they've already compared the current series to making three movies a year. Meanwhile, *Sherlock*'s fourth and fifth series are already being planned, though an official announcement and release date must wait for the main actors' schedules to be confirmed. More intriguingly, those series have actually been plotted out:

> "Rather excitingly, Mark [Gatiss] and I, for no particular reason, we just got out of the rain and sat at the top of the [Sherlock] production bus and we just started plotting out what we could do in the future," said Moffat. "And we plotted out the whole of series four and five.
>
> "So we have got plans - but our plans don't tend to be, 'Let's blow up the world or cast the most famous person in the world', they tend to be, 'What exciting twists and turns can we add to this?' And I think we've got some crackers.
> "The ideas we had that day, I thought, were the best we've ever had." (Fletcher)

Sherlock's third series broke DVD pre-order records for a season still being aired. The boxset of *Sherlock* series 1 and 2 took a place in the top ten best-sellers of 2013 under TV titles. *Sherlock* conventions are happening across the world. There are new anthologies being published, and fans are making every possible shirt, badge, and piece of jewelry. Fan communities number in millions on some of the most popular social media sites. Thus in just a few episodes the new series has redefined Sherlock Holmes as well as fandom forever.

SHERLOCK

Actors

Benedict Cumberbatch	Sherlock Holmes
Martin Freeman	Dr. John Watson
Rupert Graves	DI Greg Lestrade
Una Stubbs	Mrs. Hudson
Mark Gatiss	Mycroft Holmes
Jonathan Aris	DI Anderson
Louise Brealey	Molly Hooper
David Nellist	Mike Stamford
Zoe Telford	Sarah Sawyer
Andrew Scott	Jim Moriarty
Lara Pulver	Irene Adler
Wanda Ventham	Mrs. Holmes
Timothy Carlton	Mr. Holmes, Sr.
Amanda Abbington	Mary Morstan
Lars Mikkelsen	Charles A. Magnussen

Writers

Mark Gatiss	(9 episodes, pilot and webisode)
Steven Moffat	(9 episodes, pilot and webisode)
Arthur Conan Doyle	(credited for 9 episodes)
Steve Thompson	(3 episodes)

Executive Producers

Mark Gatiss
Steven Moffat
Sue Vertue
Beryl Vertue
Rebecca Eaton (Masterpiece)
Bethan Jones (BBC)

SHERLOCK

Works Cited

Adams, Guy. *The Sherlock Files: The Official Companion to the Hit Television Series.* USA: It Books, 2013.

Doyle, Sir Arthur Conan. *The Complete Sherlock Holmes.* http://sherlock-holm.es/stories/html/cano.html

Fletcher, Alex. "Sherlock Series 4 and 5 Already 'Plotted Out', Says Steven Moffat." *Digital Spy* Jan 9 2014. http://www.digitalspy.com/british-tv/s129/sherlock/news/a542627/sherlock-series-4-and-5-already-plotted-out-says-steven-moffat.html#ixzz2q9z263av

Gatiss, Mark. "Sherlock Series Three: New Details Revealed." *Telegraph* 3 May 2012. http://www.telegraph.co.uk/culture/tvandradio/9243417/Sherlock-series-three-new-details-revealed.html

Jeffery, Morgan. "Sherlock: Lars Mikkelsen Terrifying as New Villain, Says Steven Moffat." *Digital Spy* 9 Jan 2004. http://www.digitalspy.com/british-tv/s129/sherlock/news/a542723/sherlock-lars-mikkelsen-terrifying-as-new-villain-says-steven-moffat.html#ixzz2q8gex96M

Jeffery, Morgan and Tom Mansell. "'Sherlock' Star Andrew Scott: 'It's very Hard for Moriarty to Return'." *Digital Spy* 22 May 2012. http://www.digitalspy.com/british-tv/s129/sherlock/news/a382182/sherlock-star-andrew-scott-its-very-hard-for-moriarty-to-return.html#ixzz2pvbpMAfi

Penny, Laurie. "Sherlock and the Adventure of the Overzealous Fanbase." *New Statesman* 12 January 2014. http://www.newstatesman.com/culture/2014/01/sherlock-and-adventure-overzealous-fanbase

Sherlock: Season One. BBC Home Entertainment, 2011. DVD.

Sherlock: Season Two. BBC Home Entertainment, 2012. DVD.

SwanPride. "Symbolism in The Reichenbach Fall." Blog Post. 17 Aug 2013. http://swanpride.livejournal.com/15582.html#cutid1

BBC Websites

The Science of Deduction | www.thescienceofdeduction.co.uk
John Watson's Blog | www.johnwatsonblog.co.uk
Molly Hooper's Diary | www.mollyhooper.co.uk
Connie Prince's official site | www.connieprince.co.uk
The websites were written by Joseph Lidster.

The Whip Hand | twitter.com/#!/thewhiphand
The Twitter feed was created by Hartswood Films.

With thanks to Ariane DeVere for her wonderful *Sherlock* transcripts at arianedevere.livejournal.com.

Index

About the Author

Valerie Estelle Frankel is the author of many nonfiction books:

- ❖ *Buffy and the Heroine's Journey*
- ❖ *From Girl to Goddess: The Heroine's Journey in Myth and Legend*
- ❖ *Katniss the Cattail: An Unauthorized Guide to Names and Symbols in The Hunger Games*
- ❖ *The Many Faces of Katniss Everdeen: Exploring the Heroine of The Hunger Games*
- ❖ *Harry Potter, Still Recruiting: An Inner Look at Harry Potter Fandom*
- ❖ *Teaching with Harry Potter*
- ❖ *Myths and Motifs in The Mortal Instruments*
- ❖ *Winter is Coming: Symbols, Portents, and Hidden Meanings in A Game of Thrones*
- ❖ *Winning the Game of Thrones: The Host of Characters and their Agendas*
- ❖ *Doctor Who and the Hero's Journey: The Doctor and Companions as Chosen Ones*
- ❖ *Doctor Who: The What Where and How*

Once a lecturer at San Jose State University, she's a frequent speaker on fantasy, myth, pop culture, and the heroine's journey and can be found at http://vefrankel.com.

CPSIA information can be obtained at www.ICGtesting.com
Printed in the USA
LVOW05s2151271114

415968LV00014B/346/P